OUT OF LINE

Other Books by Tanis MacDonald

POETRY
Fortune
Holding Ground
Rue the Day

NON-FICTION
The Daughter's Way: Canadian Women's Paternal Elegies

OUT OF LINE

Daring to be an Artist
Outside the Big City

Tanis MacDonald

WOLSAK
& WYNN

Cover and interior design: Marijke Friesen
Author photograph: John Roscoe
Typeset in Minion
Printed by Ball Media, Brantford, Canada

The publisher gratefully acknowledges the support of the Canada Council for the Arts, the Ontario Arts Council and the Government of Canada.

Wolsak and Wynn Publishers
280 James Street North
Hamilton, ON
Canada L8R 2L3

Library and Archives Canada Cataloguing in Publication

MacDonald, Tanis, 1962–, author
    Out of line : daring to be an artist outside the big city / Tanis MacDonald.

Includes bibliographical references.
ISBN 978-1-928088-59-2 (softcover)

    I. Title.

PS8575.D6657O98 2018   C814'.54   C2018-900559-9

For my students

Look round, then, and see that none of the uninitiated is listening. The uninitiated are those who believe in nothing but what they can grasp in their hands, and who deny the existence of actions and generation and all that is invisible.

– Plato, *Theaetetus*

TABLE OF CONTENTS

Preface

How do you establish and sustain an artistic practice when the circumstances of your life seem to oppose it? Or, put more plainly, how do you make art when you come from an artless place?

"Artless" is relative, of course: a place where art is not central, let's say, or a place where art is starved to thinness, or shoved in a corner and told to behave. I thought about this off and on for many years as I wrote poems, then books, then designed and taught courses, then published literary criticism. I thought about it as I moved across Canada several times in pursuit of degrees and jobs and community. As social media ramped up, fostering a hyper-performative and omnipresent pressure to position oneself as a writer, I thought about those of us who live far from big arts communities and still make art, and that led me to think about privilege and obscurity and inclusiveness. Mostly I thought about it here, in a small city surrounded by farmland where factories were shutting down, as I taught creative writing courses to people who were craving a way to think of themselves as artists and writers. I saw hunger and apprehension in their faces: it was very familiar. They looked like I did a few decades ago, and like I sometimes felt now. It was like looking into a mirror. In that same small city, far from both my home place and the Big City, I remembered reading Mark Zuehlke and Louise Donnelly's short instructive book *Magazine Writing from the Boonies* back in 1997, when I still lived in Toronto, and knew that the years and the miles had remade me into what Zuehlke and Donnelly call a "boonie writer": someone who maintained an artistic practice far from the madding literary crowd.

There can be no question that technology has changed things in the years since that book was published. Email and websites and social media in all its forms have made the "boonies" relative: so far and yet so electronically near. But the day-to-day, feet-on-the-ground artmaking thrives on in-person contact, and as time went by, I had to think seriously about what it is to make yourself (and remake yourself) as a practitioner of art far from a big cultural centre. I could see that my students, in literature courses and in creative writing courses, wanted answers about how they might enter the writing life. My own recalibrated questions about the pleasures and problems of small-place art creation dovetailed with their concerns.

Because the moment the students and I started discussing how to begin, the relative distance between our small place and the Big City ballooned, and the instantaneity of the Internet became largely irrelevant. My students saw right through the veil of accessibility provided by the Internet and got straight to the heart of the matter: how to make art here, with what was before them right now, not in a future that they could not see and a place that they could not (yet) imagine. The ease of blogging and online curation notwithstanding, beginner writers of all ages still crave answers about what it is to have a creative community, and further, a creative practice. These were good things to want to know, and I began to feel my own beginnings as a writer surfacing in my memory as I worked through some answers with my students. How did I figure out that an artistic practice was worth developing and maintaining? Making art of any kind was not an idea that I had picked up from my mostly lower-middle-class friends in my uncool suburb on the edge of the Prairies where I lived with my Depression-era-raised parents. So who made the pursuit of creating things a possibility for me? The term *artistic practice* can seem pretentious, especially if you have a working-class background like I do. But I mean something doable and even measurable; in the ordinary course of a life, beyond high-flown ideas of awards or public adoration, an artistic practice is what you do to make stuff. Are you a musician? What's the last concert you saw? When did you last play with someone else? What's the last piece you learned? Are you a writer? What are you reading? When did you last write something for yourself? When did you last return to a draft and work to make it better? When was the last time you referred to yourself as a musician or a writer in public? These questions illustrate some of the ways that the work of making something (and admitting to making something) takes repetitive and material practice: time spent when it may appear to others that you are doing nothing useful. If you are from a working-class background or even one generation away from it, you will hear about "usefulness" a lot. An artistic practice, among others things, is rooted in the belief that practice is useful.

The development of an artistic practice is an oddly kept secret, buoyed by a strong cultural belief in instant genius or overnight success. It's no secret, of course, to people in MFA programs or those with strong creative communities, but for many who are beginner artists, this seems as alien and far from them as the moon. For instance, in the imaginations of many people, writers sit in a garret and derive their brilliance from their refusal of the workaday world. They live in big cities without mundane concerns, write furiously in cafés and then spend hours talking to their brilliant friends, arguing passionately into the night. But what if that isn't your life? What if you are trying to write in a lonely environment, trying to create in a small community? Beginner artists can sometimes talk themselves out of developing an artistic practice because their surroundings don't fit any picture of an artistic life that they've ever seen. But the truth about most writers' lives is much more complicated and much more interesting than starving in a garret or composing in cafés. Writers create art not despite the world's presence, but because they live in the world, and because the world works on them.

Out of Line is about how to begin functioning as an artist if you haven't been raised to think of art as something made by people you know and therefore makable by you. What would it be like to nurture artmaking as an active practice? It is also a book about starting and continuing as a writer outside of a large urban centre. I hope to give you a way to begin at the beginning when your background is artistically inauspicious and you are "out of line" with your family, your class, your background and the Big Events happening elsewhere. This is a book about grounding your creativity and establishing your community; working with, not despite, your uncool background; and about all the barriers, naysayers, reasons to write and *not* to write that you may encounter on the way.

The phrase *out of line* as the title of this book does triple duty as a metaphor: first, to gesture to the quest for artistic practices and community by people who are living "out of line," far from an artistic hot spot. Second, the title alludes to the beginner artist's choice to defy social expectations: to step away from accepted behaviours in our small-place or suburban contexts, and make art despite being told that "you can't," "you shouldn't" and "why would you want to do *that*?" The third meaning for "out of line" is more nefarious, and equally necessary to address: it connotes how mentors with power sometimes depend upon the naïveté of beginners with outsider backgrounds, and use this vulnerability to take advantage of beginner artists. While I chose the title wanting to tap its geographical and social defiance, I would be remiss if I did not discuss this shadow across our artistic communities in a larger consideration about the importance of a cohort.

This book will address some issues of class, but the best book I know about class is *Where We Stand: Class Matters* by the African-American feminist, cultural critic and social activist bell hooks, and I recommend it to you. In that book, hooks describes the landscape of privilege at the intersections of race, gender and class, and warns that we consider class difference too little, especially in our educational institutions. *Out of Line* is not a book about academic study, but the university classroom will come up occasionally as one kind of training ground for artists and the milieu in which I encounter beginner artists most often. In *Where We Stand*, hooks acknowledges a hard truth about being working class in the academy, what she calls the "price of the ticket." We are expected to leave the past – that is, our backgrounds – behind. As hooks says: "Poor students would be welcome at the best institutions of higher learning only if they were willing to surrender memory, to forget the past and claim the assimilated present as the only worthwhile and meaningful reality." She also notes that given this kind of pressure, many students cannot "bear the weight of all the contradictions they had to confront." I have experienced this as a professor and as a student, and one of the reasons I wrote this book was to open up discussion among my students and other beginner artists about what artists' lives are really like, and to say that an artistic practice and artistic community are practical tools in resisting assimilation, in the university, in publishing, in the world.

The awkwardness of discussing class and the arts community is a serious matter. I asked my friends and colleagues about their early education and beliefs about what art was and who gets to make it, the niches they have found or made for themselves and the communities in which they have participated.

The responses, from these colleagues and others whose words will appear throughout *Out of Line*, suggest that most mid-life artists are very aware of the chances that did not come their way and the ones that did. They remember the people who told them one thing that made a difference or advised them in a way that changed everything. Over and over, I read responses from artists who felt as though an ordinary life just missed them, that it whizzed by as they stepped "out of line" to do something different. Several people wrote that they just squeaked through with their oddness due to someone's good advice or timely help, very often offered casually but at a crucial moment. Such timely help can take all kinds of forms. This book offers said help in practical chapters, goofy (but true) anecdotes, lyric prose and personal essays: a collage of experiences. Some of these pieces will resemble literary tear sheets, out-of-line asides that don't summarize as much as blur the boundaries between advice and experience. We are all in this long making game together, and some pieces in *Out of Line* act as beacons from the beyond of my creative practice, or, in the words of Joan Hotchkis, as letters I didn't send home.

There are a lot of instructional books on writing that you could read, all of them intriguingly packed with exercises and advice on how to get words on a page. I have a whole shelf of these books and often consult them. This will not be one of those books, useful though they are. I am going to trust that you are already getting words on a page, or trying to, and acquainting yourself with practice as both fascination and frustration. Instead of writing instruction, I want to reveal some of the less-discussed fundaments of an artistic practice that my students always ask about: "How do I find people to talk to about writing?" "How do I keep writing outside of class?" "Can I be a writer if I don't have that kind of background?" And most practically and poignantly: "How do I do this?"

Let's find out.

This is for You

This is for you, sitting in the back of your high school class, or maybe in the front, bored and barely passing or passing without trying and wondering why it all seems so formulaic. This is for you in the library, reading anything and everything you can get your hands on not because you are so fascinated, though you might be sometimes, but because you never know what book might give you that sliver of light, the key to getting out of this place, this school, this set of expectations. This is for you who goes to church or temple or gurdwara at your parents' insistence and gets lost for a moment or two in the rhythm of the words or music or prayers or readings, or the harmonies of hymns you haven't believed in for years but still, they sound like leaving, like art that gets made somewhere far away from here. This is for you working that job you wanted, or that job you needed to pay the bills, still thinking about the key to getting out of this place, but you don't want out – you only want more of what you get when you pick up a pen or a paintbrush or a sander, here in this place.

This is for you, your hidden weirdo glory in your rural community, your town without a theatre, your small city with no writers, your family who just wants you to study science and be a doctor who can move back home and serve the community. And yes, you agree in principle, that would be good, but. For you in the suburbs, so close and yet so far from all the lights and colours, from the dancing, from art and its makers. This is for you, backstage crew too cool and afraid to go on stage in the high school play, and you're more into Zeppelin anyway, man. For you, yearbook staff, town headbanger, geek girl, girly boy, boyly girl, young poets and painters, people who want to dance but don't know how, class clown and the shyest person in school, the one who says "journalist" so you don't have to explain "writer"; who says "commercial artist" to excuse your compulsive drawing, and so you don't have to say that you really want to leave this place and live in a garret far far away. For you, who wants to read Toni Morrison or Eden Robinson or Ursula K. Le Guin for your book club, or go into the Big City to see the Frida Kahlo exhibit and don't know what to say when people ask, "Why would you want to do that?"

This is for you, first generation of your family to go to university with the weight of that privilege and expectation, all that money spent on you, all that guilt, all that future to fill, and you know you'll have to pay somehow, but how? This is for you, thinking you're too old to take a class now that you are thirty-five, forty-five or fifty-five.

I see you making art out of almost nothing, out of your sheer will to make something of your own, something different from what you see every day. I see you finding books; I see you sewing and singing and making collages, staying late in art class, playing the piano for Sunday school. I see you playing D&D and Second Life and RPGs for the pleasure of becoming someone else, and you are relieved that you don't have to call it art and be shamed for it. I see you cooking and baking for the pleasure of making; I see you learning the names of birds and plants for their mellifluous, tongue-tripping beauty; I see you mucking out a calf's stall for the sweet smell of hay and baby animal shit, for the calf's tangle of limbs in the morning. I see you running to listen to the rhythm of your breath, that heart music. I see you learning to speak the language of your ancestors. I see you saying the word *ancestors* with a dawning sense of your history.

I see you saying nothing when someone calls you a dreamer or a pansy or a fag or an airhead; a fluffball, a slut, a flake or just an idiot for thinking you could be more, do more, catch beauty in a jar, get out of this place, be something other than. I am thinking of you making art in unlikely and sometimes stringent circumstances: writing on your lunch hour, or taking photos with your phone, or curating books and films and paintings to declare what you love, or saving old beautiful things from the landfill, or kerning the lettering on an event poster. Special shout-out to those of you who have to listen to people all day telling you that it's not art, that it's banal, that it's more useless information, that the care you take and attention you give will add up to nothing. I will tell you this one thing in hope that it will help sustain you: you know what needs doing.

I see you, fat or bone-thin or just ordinary invisible; I see you with your perfect skin that will never be perfect enough; I see you rebel with every cause that you are not going to speak to because what's the point, who would hear you, Cassandra, Philomela, Tiresias; I see you getting a little older and a little older still; I see you push back against the beast; I hear you fight to breathe, clawing your way out of that lonely purgatory you fell into three or four or ten years ago when he hit you, or she left, or everyone laughed and never let you forget. I see you washing the dishes or mowing the lawn while he jeers, while she tells you that you are never leaving, while he says that he's the boss and can do whatever he wants to you. I see you, and I tell you that you deserve a life, a way out; you deserve your body and brain working in concert with all the art ever made – every piece of music, every brush stroke, every high note, every leap into the air; every curve, muscle, swing, colour, shape and shadow. Every word.

Portraits of the Artists as Young Artsies

The transformation of silence into language and action is an act
of self-revelation, and that always seems fraught with danger.
– Audre Lorde, *Sister Outsider*

Every day, people make choices that work for their circumstances,
which can include some or all of the following: the need to earn
money, to stay safe, to raise children or care for the vulnerable, to
advocate for justice, to pay rent, to eat, to learn other skills or ideas,
to obtain a professional qualification and/or to respond to rapid
change. Because these are real-life no-messing-around demands,
the dream of the Big City art life has to remain a dream for some.
But an artistic practice doesn't strictly need an urban context, and
though that transformation from silence to language can seem
fraught with danger, as Lorde notes, self-revelation can happen
wherever you push against expectation. Sometimes those expectations are personal and sometimes they are cultural. The T-shirts
that engineering students sometimes wear, declaring "Friends don't

let Friends become Artsies," should be reckoned against all the people who STEMed their way through life before deciding in their forties or fifties that their life really should have been dedicated to poetry, or the theatre, or painting. We should reclaim the term *Artsy* because there would be no culture without people who take time from all their other responsibilities to devote themselves to art. We should not let ourselves be disdained. We perform very valuable public functions, quite aside from making art. Artsies relieve people of the need to read everything. We're the ones who obsess over harmonies or colour blends: we remember important dates and who wrote what.

Artsies are the makers of order where there is chaos. At a party, we might stay in a corner of the room, though anyone who invests in the cliché that all Artsies are introverts should watch poets dance. Granted, we are not always in the centre of things because we have other fish to fry; we are usually thinking of the next hour that we will have entirely to ourselves, to write down what we just saw or heard, or to draw it, paint it, sing it, play it, arrange and arrange and rearrange components endlessly on the page, screen, in our heads. Eventually, people will say to us, "How did you do that?" Or "How did you know that?" Or more simply, "Get out of my head." If you live with an Artsy, get used to the sound of something brewing. To most people, it will sound like silence. You may be asked, "What is up with your in-house Artsy?" You don't have to answer. Especially if you are the in-house Artsy.

The Artsy comes in all shapes and sizes and colours and ages and genders and sexes and cultures and backgrounds and ambitions and educations and desires and social classes. "How do I become a writer?" my students ask, a question reflected infinitely on social media by people older than my students – some with books, some without, some jockeying for position in the spring and fall book seasons, some arguing about style and coteries and reviewing, some braving the hard truths about sexism and racism and violence. These are conversations by, for and about people who are fiercely devoted to ideas of what a writer could be or should be. Who is doing the work? Who is acknowledged as having done the work? Is the role of writer or artist changing in response to our world? There can never be one answer to this. In fact, the world in which there is only one answer to this is a world from which I would run screaming.

When I first saw Wes Anderson's *Rushmore*, I could not stop thinking that I was Max Fischer, only he had much more money and an Ivy League prep school backing him. That movie was about how Max didn't fit in, and I liked it – the mad genius plans, the over-the-top production values – even as I disbelieved every frame. His privilege was overwhelming to me. I know Wes Anderson writes elaborate fantasies, and that watching them and expecting realism is really not the way to get the most out of one of his films. This movie remains one of my favourites because of my disbelief, rather than in spite of it. It's classic wish fulfillment in Technicolor. No one would have made a movie about my art-geek life in high school, and I'll bet no one made one out of yours either. If you spend much time thinking about this, the ways that unspoken class privilege looms large in arts industries becomes clear: that almost immeasurable but definite whiff of the right to be here, the ability to attend the right events in the right place with the right people, where the right people you met at some other event introduce you to someone else who gives you your "big break."

Writers dream of that cliché, too, as starry-eyed in our ways as anyone who has lit out for Hollywood, each of us thinking our own version of "and when my book's published, I'll be famous and admired!" Most of us won't admit to that because striving is uncool, as is ambition, as is sounding like you care. But my position as Duchess of the Perpetually Uncool grants me special powers, so I'm saying it. If you've been in the literary world for decades, or grew up in it, you might bristle at the idea and object to this as an unfair characterization of your social life. Maybe so, but when you are an outsider, everything looks like a barrier designed to keep you out. This may or may not be a version of the garrison mentality, but it is definitely a manifestation of being out of line.

Poet and non-fiction writer Maureen Hynes lays it out plainly: "I do strongly believe class is a crucial factor, like gender, race, ethnicity, sexual orientation and ability (and how these commonly intersect with each other), in how comfortable people feel in entering a room of strangers, introducing oneself to others, in sharing written work or even speaking up in a class. In feeling like you have a place in this community and that people understand and accept who you are. In my work in the labour movement, I saw how deep-seated the intimidation, the mistrust or fear of education can be, how the educational system has a capacity to brutalize even the brightest of working-class children." Writer Liz Ukrainetz notes that a working-class background estranges people from "the cultural alphabet of the shapes and gestures of places, ideas and values," and that though she "received them peripherally through the cultural soup – *Star Trek*, Roger Ramjet, the Jackson Five, the Who . . . the difference between living beside a language, and living in it, is large."

Learning to make art – or learning to trust that you are making art – when you come from an artless place is not easy. In the hits and misses, we find the shape of our practice. But if you are coming from a place where art is not valued, or perhaps not recognized, it may not be so simple. Juno-winning dub poet and performer Lillian Allen, who has mentored hundreds of young artists, has the best advice for taking your own creative temperature: "your art will never be enough, but if you feel like nothing will be enough without you developing a practice and living a creative life, then you are already an artist." Poet and visual artist derek beaulieu contributed this quotation from visual artist Sister Corita Kent: "Find a place you can trust and then try trusting it for a while."

It takes commitment to make your own artistic community, but people do it all the time. A quick look at writing communities across Canada yields many examples, including people who have built their communities within larger centres that demanded a more assimilative expression. One of the first poems I ever heard Lillian Allen perform was "Nelly Belly Swelly" at the World of Music, Arts, and Dance Festival at the Shipdeck Stage at Toronto's Harbourfront in 1988. It was my first experience with dub poetry. Lillian owned the stage; she was mesmerizing. A few years later, when I had started to write, I saw a notice for the launch of her book *Women Do This Every Day* at the Poor Alex in Toronto's Annex, and I went, craving more of her voice and confidence. That was the night I heard her perform "One Poem Town," a poem in which Lillian unpacked the whiteness of the Toronto literary scene and I was amazed that someone could do that: work in the scene, criticize it and make one's own art at the same time. I was a bit old for this kind of awakening, but it was a lesson I would need to learn again and again. She was completely right about the narrowness of the literary scene, but I had never heard anyone say it aloud before and I started to think about my own narrow definitions of writing. If Lillian was out there, working and changing things, who else was? Who else had I missed because, like the working-class girl I am, I was so focused on conventionality?

My experience of hearing Lillian happened in a big city, but it just as easily could have happened in a smaller place: in fact, smaller places offer these kinds of challenges to "mainstreamed" culture all the time, often by virtue of being geographically isolated. For instance, Halifax has a thriving spoken word scene led by former Municipal

Poet El Jones and current Municipal Poet Rebecca Thomas, both with powerful feminist voices and strong roots in their communities. Jones and Thomas make it their business to create socially conscious art that discusses Black lives and Mi'kmaq lives on the East Coast. In Kitchener-Waterloo, Janice Lee, Beth Murch, Bashar Jabbour and Ashley Hommel-Hynd draw the crowds at KW Poetry Slam, bringing in guest readers from all across Canada. Lee's 2018 film *The Legend of Sing Hey* is a documentary about her search throughout Canada for writers and musicians who are Black, Indigenous and People of Colour (BIPOC), often finding them living as artmakers in small centres. If you've not encountered it before, the term *BIPOC* is very useful; it gestures to structural inequities shared by people with these identities yet it also separates and differentiates those communities and their histories. It's similar in some ways to how the term *LGBTQ* indicates solidarity among lesbian, gay, bisexual, transgender and queer folks without implying that their politics or challenges are exactly the same. And across Canada, other out-of-line places have found ways to bring together writers to practice arts in grassroots, self-generated communities. In Winnipeg, Cree writer Duncan Mercredi and a long list of Indigenous writers have been meeting to write and mentor young writers via the Indigenous Writers Collective since the 1980s. Further north, Saskatchewan Poet Laureate Brenda Schmidt runs a northern reading series in Flin Flon, Manitoba, called Ore Samples, in honour of the city's mining heritage. Calgary has fostered enough experimental and avant-garde writers in the last two decades that derek beaulieu and rob mclennan brought them all together in an anthology called, with sly seriousness, *The Calgary Renaissance*. For ten years, on Vancouver's Downtown Eastside, the Thursdays Writing Collective brought together a diverse group of people from the neighbourhood and beyond to write and create a literary community, coordinated by Amber Dawn and Elee Kraljii Gardiner. In

Victoria, Planet Earth Poetry continues to bring together a diverse group of writers, including guests from all over the country.

But even with all this evidence of small-place arts communities, the dynamics of belonging and not belonging are complex. How do we begin? Sometimes we just want to know if what we want is even possible. Whitehorse writer Joanna Lilley noted that when she first started writing, she "wanted to know that I wasn't being ridiculous, audacious or pretentious to dream that I could be a writer. I wanted to know how to do it. How to magically transform myself into someone who was worthy enough and skilled enough to have my name on a book. How did one learn to write? I wanted to know it was okay to say out loud that I wanted to be a writer but I don't think I even had the confidence to articulate that question." Confidence is key, and so is environment, and sometimes you can't control either. Poet and novelist Jeanette Lynes was acutely aware that her early education in visual art wouldn't get her into a university program to study more – not for lack of trying, but "a rural high school couldn't provide up-to-the-minute art instruction. I loved colour, and would have benefitted from colour theory, and more instruction but resources for this were not available in Grey County, or, at least none that I knew of. Geographical isolation was a big factor."

Sometimes being first-generation Canadian, or a first-generation artist of any kind, comes with the price of estrangement from art that is rooted in cultural tradition. Songwriter and poet Janice Lee notes: "I never read my mom's poetry because it was in Korean and my Korean was not good enough to understand it." Writer and spoken word artist Meharoona Ghani saw art rooted in language and female social practice: "At times, my mother sang songs in our language. She played a dholki (a South Asian drum) for wedding parties. I viewed her as an artist…I remember going to 'ladies' parties' associated with South Asian weddings where there was a lot of traditional dance and singing. Found these to be fun. Community driven. Woman driven.

Women empowered." Ghani adds that the consumerism of these arts (in both the northern and southern hemispheres) spurred her to take them up in order to return them to their roots. Observing the appropriation of henna and Indian classical dance by consumers of diverse backgrounds, Ghani notes, "we saw how our long-held arts were being used by folks to make money out of it."

Jane Eaton Hamilton, writer and photographer, reminded me that a change in physical capacity is an often-overlooked reason to become an artist: "I wouldn't have been an artist at all if I had not become disabled, but rather a scientist working in animal communication. Writing would have remained an occasional hobby." Kim Clark also noted that experiencing physical changes in her body brought her to art: "I was diagnosed with MS at forty-three. An uncertain future with progressing disability drove me back to high school, college and to university for a degree based on the gonzo idea and pursuit of writing because, I thought, 'What else will I physically be able to do, while dispelling the myth that was me?'" But for all the sense of discovery in art as a way to extend a body beyond its limitations, Hamilton notes that with those limitations, real-world marginalization from community often follows: "My disability, besides having an impact on my finances, also meant I couldn't attend the workshops and classes where other writers met mentors/built connections to last them a lifetime." Memoirist and activist Dorothy Palmer agrees: "Currently, my biggest obstacle is the pervasive, systemic ableism of CanLit culture. The expectation of being able-bodied is built right into the writing life, a requirement to network, promote and publicize your book." The expectation of having time, money and the ability to travel to research, network or promote your work is an assumption of privilege and adds an extra distance to life as an out-of-line artist.

You can see that people in all kinds of circumstances and with all kinds of backgrounds have already figured out ways to make lives that sustain the making of art, and that begins in many ways with a focus on what it could look like to start here and now. Training programs are great, but what is necessary for us all is to place ourselves at the centre of the inquiry into forging an artistic practice. I like the way that poet (and my former student) Kyleen McGragh puts it: "What do I have to teach myself?" To offer a personal example, I can still see the paper from the Sage Hill Writing Retreat that arrived at my Toronto apartment in 1995, which noted this as the first item on a list of advice: "Develop an appetite for revision." In my memory, the words glow and pulse on the page, though of course that is merely a fanciful image that I've polished over time. But that phrasing dug in for me: I liked that I didn't have to be good at it or have the right references or have read the right books or have someone powerful (oh my God, who?) advocate for me. All I had to do was learn to crave revision the way I craved a million other things that were beyond my star. I read that sentence and smiled. I was made of craving, and I could learn to crave revision.

*

Considering the process as a reward is decent advice, especially when you are starting out, because the rewards will be few at first: intelligent eyes on your work, someone who says, "this is good!" or a reading or installation or performance with a small audience. Practicing patience with yourself will bolster you in lean times, and there are always going to be lean times, financially or psychologically. My instructors and mentors and senior peers advised – strongly – that we feed our artistic practices and not our often-fragile egos. When you are beginning, this can be a fine distinction. But if the process were all the reward anyone needed, why would anyone publish? Sing for an audience? Act in a play? For me, seven books in and with twenty-five years of magazine and journal publishing, I will say that having faith in an audience is a skill. Everyone needs their own proportion of process and audience. I don't know what your proportion will be like, but you can reasonably expect it to shift throughout your artistic life. When you are a beginner artist, the shock of having an audience can be as great as the delight of it.

An extremely smart friend once told me that she was trying to calculate what kind of encouragement and approbation would be enough for her. She pictured a concert scenario: a stadium of people cheering, howling their approval, roaring out their love for her and her work; and even as she pictured it, she thought, "it's not enough." She also knew that the chances of her getting that arena full of people cheering were slim; she wasn't a rock star or a professional athlete. Sometimes we write for love, for approval or for admiration. This is may not be 100 per cent psychologically healthy, but it is perfectly normal. There needs to be something else driving your art, because not everyone will love your work and not everyone will approve of or admire you. Some people may even think your work is bad. Others may sit up and take notice; they may say, "Wait – what's this?" when they read what you've written. And that's who you are looking for, and who you are writing to, at least at the start: your people, your peers, your readers.

If you grew up like Lena Dunham, the offspring of radical artists, or even just in a house with lots of books and art and tickets to concerts and plays, you've probably met your fair share of artists, and the mystery of how to be one was answered for you early. But if you grew up like I did, in a small town or a culturally squeezed suburb, and have just started to think about how to see more art so you can make more art, it's possible you've never met an actor or a painter or someone who says that they publish poetry. Sometimes I catch beginner writers watching me in my alienness. I know that my ordinary exterior tests their belief in what an artist looks and sounds like. This feeling of being under a microscope comes with the territory; it happens all the time to artists who work as instructors, but it also happens to any artist who is generous with their time. I come under a certain kind of scrutiny because I may be the first published writer some of my students have met, though I rarely seem "writerly." This could mean any number of things, but it starts with the fact that I look – how shall I say this accurately and with kindness? – unremarkable. I'm white, middle-aged and cisgendered. I am not glamorous. Perhaps it is most accurate to say that I don't look much like a culturally approved image of a female artist. It is a truth annoyingly and universally acknowledged that male writers can look like they live on beer and pickles and haven't bought shoes in a decade or more, but female writers (especially when they appear in public) had better dress and photograph like models. There is a good deal of performing writerliness that happens in arts communities, and this too often relies on rules of attractiveness, ability and normativity in ways that reduce the potential for the art to speak to the realities of people's lives. Because it ought to be all about the art. The Duchess of Uncoolness speaks: it is a function of my experience and my privilege, as someone who makes most of their income from teaching, that I don't enact many of those performances anymore. I perform writing by writing, or by talking to other people about their writing. I sometimes think beginner writers are waiting for my bland exterior to melt away and reveal the leather-clad, long-haired, chain-smoking artist within. Artists don't need to dress in any special way, and bestselling authors usually resemble rumpled people who sit in front of a keyboard for eight hours a day: bad backs, taut Achilles tendons, loose mud-coloured clothing. If you have the confidence to sign your art on your body in some way, it can draw other artists to you like a lighthouse beacon. Your courage can embolden others in a small community, or a new community.

At one point in time, I was gloriously pretentious, and if you've read this far, you have earned a story about my youthful artistic pretension. My errors are only good for the examples that they provide;

they are otherwise sitting around doing nothing. I was eighteen and fresh from acting in a string of semi-professional local productions when I met my friend W. I saw a play he was performing in, and because I was full of overweening self-confidence, I went backstage to introduce myself. *How* full of overweening self-confidence? I told W that I was an actor myself and I really enjoyed his performance. This was true enough, though all about me: offering a review like he was dying for my good opinion. For what it's worth, I had enjoyed his performance; he was easily the funniest actor in the show. The play was *Enter Laughing*, and W was much funnier in a secondary role than the lead guy playing the young comedian. Having made my pronouncement from on high to the stunned but complemented W, I then made a dramatic exit in a swirl of whatever flowing get-up I had effected that week and disappeared into the night. I met W again a month later, at the start of the university term, when we ended up in the same theatre history class. I waved at him across the room and his brow furrowed. When the class ended, he appeared at my elbow and said, "I thought you were an actor. But you're just a kid like me." Caught in my own pretensions but still determined to define myself as an artist, I replied: "I am an actor – and I'm a kid like you." When I think about it now, I feel equal parts embarrassment at my pretentiousness and pride at my strong sense of artistic selfhood. I knew that if I was going to make any kind of attempt to get the hell outta Dodge, I needed practice. W was my friend for the next fifteen years, until he died when we were both just thirty-three. He was way too young, but this was during the era of the AIDS epidemic. I miss him and how he would laugh when he told the story of how we met, which he did whenever anyone asked. It's good to have friends who have known you for a long time and don't hate you for your errors. It's good to have community.

A Manifesto

I have a very modest artistic manifesto. I wanted to figure out how things happen.

*

No, that's not entirely right. I wanted to be accurate about what I saw, but I found everything so slippery. Even solid objects had too many sides. There was always a thing beyond a thing that I couldn't get the words around.

*

I wanted to record. I thought that if I didn't record a particular moment it would go unremembered, or worse, that it would be as though it had not happened. Kids are natural existentialists – at least I was. I was eight when I stood on the front steps of my house on Waverley Street, watching an old turquoise car with a rounded hood making a rattling noise as it clunked through the potholes of our street, and I thought that I needed to remember this, because no one else was there on the steps with me and no one else had seen it. Because it might be important, even though I didn't and couldn't know how.

*

That is it. That little moment and my accompanying thought are all I can offer as an originary aesthetic moment. Non-spoiler alert: the car didn't turn out to be important in any way, and it doesn't symbolize anything in particular. It's a slow eyeblink of a moment, and the awareness of that moment as a possibility of artmaking. I don't have a story about how or why I became a writer; some people have that moment, and I have the moment with the turquoise car, which isn't a story at all. Other writers have more narratively driven awakening stories: for example, someone might learn to write narrative through writing letters to their faraway cousin and recounting the events of the day, and someone else might learn to write dialogue from listening to their parents fight. I worry, sometimes, that if our artistic awakening stories aren't sense-making or dramatic, if they aren't elevator-pitch-perfect, they will be discounted or dismissed.

My moment with the turquoise car is pretty flat. It isn't intended to inspire; I don't expect people to relate to it, though some might. I write it here precisely because of its flatness, or its refusal to offer inspiration or meaning to anyone but myself. I believe strongly in moments when everything seems to come together in one big blinding flash of politics and consciousness and aesthetics. Those moments are definitely memorable, and I am not so sure that they are the moments that forge artists. The moments that forge artists are perhaps inspired by something externally observed, but the awakenings are inevitably internal, noises heard only by the artists themselves. Artists capture unacknowledged perspectives on the ordinary that we can't always consciously grasp, so we bring them to light the outer edges of realities that we don't always occupy but are always there, pulsing when we look up. Unreality is only reality that you haven't thought yet.

*

I wanted to crush everything together. Or I wanted to write about how everything is already crushed together, a dizzying series of overlaps and conjunctions. I wanted to write a manifesto, but the density kept everything moving too quickly.

*

The manifesto I recommend to everyone thinking about art is Lynda Barry's *One! Hundred! Demons!* Barry is a multitalented writer and visual artist who made her early reputation in the underground co-mix scene of the 1980s. Her brilliant works are made of fine layers of fiction, art, autobiography and pedagogy that simply don't sep-arate. The "demons" are the googly-eyed, many-armed, slug- and bug-like monsters that Barry "calls up" and draws following the di-rections of an exercise she discovers in a book at the public library. While the creatures are "demons" in that they haunt her, they are also "daemons," advising spirits who guide the writer or philosopher throughout their life: less something to be exorcised than entities that exercise the artist. Barry's contention is that we all have such daemons, and she urges us to find our own while showing us what she did to identify hers. *One! Hundred! Demons!* is a mysterious and welcoming book. If you've never read it, I recommend it; if you've read it already, I recommend a return. The strength of the book is that Barry never says, "do this and you will get published," or "these are the best ways to write and draw." In fact, she does just the opposite. She points out that she found her way by knowing nothing, admitting it and continuing to make art anyway.

*

Knowing nothing is a great state to be in, if you can admit it. If you can't, it can be torturous. This book is not intended to instruct you about the right way to pursue art. Trends and tastes change, and there are always hundreds of ways to approach artmaking. Beginner artists are rebellious, even as they are hungry for direction; any advice I could give is something to push against as much as it is something to take up. My own practice has been varied enough that I don't especially believe in one way of doing anything, and I have a natural distrust for anyone who says "my way is the right way" in artistic practice (or politics, philosophy or religion). As far as methods go, you should learn as many of those as you can: forms and styles and traditions and histories and approaches. Lots of people can teach you, encourage you, offer tips that they have learned, advise about working in certain ways. This is a book for beginner artists, especially writers and those who feel out of line with expectations and plans, and out of the urban arts scene, creating and thinking about the dynamics of artmaking in smaller communities.

None of this will offer a magic formula for getting published. Or becoming famous. Or being loved.

Just so you know.

Out of Line in a Crowd: Communities and Cohorts

I love the title of Jeanette Winterson's terrific 2011 memoir about poverty, class, adoption, queerness and becoming a writer: *Why Be Happy When You Could Be Normal?* Winterson uses the title to ask the question every out-of-line artist will be asked. I love its queer inflection and Winterson's rejection of the "normal" in favour of happiness. I love the way the title invokes the faux-reasonable inquiry of Winterson's adoptive mother, the kind of inquiry that many of us have heard from people who want us, for reasons that may be well-intentioned or toxic, to live smaller and more regular lives. I love the call-in of this question, drawing in outcasts and misfits under the cloak of subversive resistance to "normality." Finding your people often means finding those who have dared more than you, and with good reason: knowing people who know about risk will give you courage. It is a really good idea to reconsider what your idea of community support might look like. Stepping out of line means you are going to need the assistance of people who know what it is to resist, fundamentally, profoundly, constantly. My own solidarity with LGBTQ+ people grew from my apprenticeship years, mostly because they required no explanation for my oddness when I was sixteen and looking for a place to breathe. They liked art. They didn't need me to apologize for what I liked. They weren't interested in telling anyone how to conform.

Eventually I made my escape to a big city and lived there making art in theatre and literature, not perfectly and not always for money. I had been there for nearly a decade when I attended my cousin's post-wedding party. My sense of disjunction was profound. My cousin couldn't have been more different from me and the conversations being had at the parties and dinners they held were entirely about hockey, skiing and having children. I had nothing to say about any of these subjects, and would like to claim that I acted well and with good grace, but alas, no. I didn't care about any of those things, but the biggest sin of all was that I didn't want to pretend I did. I dropped the Art Bomb. My uncle asked me what I did instead of ski or watch hockey or have children, and I said that I liked the theatre, and took poetry workshops, and read widely and knew many people who did the same – wrote, acted, danced, sang professionally, argued about poetry. The silence rippled out from there; no one knew what to say. My strangeness, mild to the point of non-existence among my current friends, was a goddamned rainbow at that dining-room table. My difference from my cousins seemed as prominent as a third eye or a pair of wings, physical attributes that everyone had spent the evening politely ignoring until I ruined everything by attempting to fly around the room.

Moments like these – and the many moments in between, when your loneliness can drive you up a wall – are why you need a community. Epiphanies and familial understanding might be within your grasp, and if they are that's excellent. But some of us don't have that and still deserve to have people in our lives who will listen, who will say, "What are you working on?" and want to know the answer.

*

Here's the thing about creative community: if you don't have it, art will break your heart. Or: if you make art and don't have community to help/share/discuss/promote/vent, the world will break your heart.

Which it may do anyway, but even broken-heartedness is better with community.

*

If you're the arts geek in your small community, that may be considered a niche of a sort. Maybe you aspire to be the person known for your art (and even mocked for it) in your smallish locale; maybe that's a step up from feeling like the art is in you but can't make it out into the world. That crammed-full feeling is frustrating, and so is feeling flattened out, emptied of possibility because there's no way the world is going to make room for you.

So knowing that feeling crammed and feeling flattened are not great ways to live a life, let's consider some other possibilities, along with their imperfections:

a) *You could change yourself.* You'll hear a lot of this one, probably in these terms: "You know that way you are? Don't be that way." Pay no attention to this.

b) *You could change places.* Go elsewhere, at least for a short while. Attending a training program of some kind (college, university, art school) is one way to do this, but alongside formal programs, there is a time-honoured tradition of moving to a big city to be an artist. People resolve to go and take any job – temping, waiting tables, bike courier – just to pay rent while they discover the city and themselves. This can depend, of course, on having the money, the confidence, and the ability and desire to leave behind obligations or attachments or opportunities at the home place.

The option that you will hear about a lot less is this:

c) *You can change your home community to be more arts accepting and arts rich.* This is doable, but requires you to be strong and to create – or find – artistic community in your home place. This is also something that people come up against when they move for work or family, as I did, or when they complete their training and return to their home place, which may be attractive for other reasons (like a lower cost of living, or proximity to family or to cultural community). Changing your home community comes with associated risks: your old friends and family who will still be present and accounted for may have plenty to say about "the change" in you, and this can be daunting. *Why are you rehearsing a play when you could be studying? What really happens at that writers' group? You're in a choir? Who told you you could sing? What's that for? What are you going to end up with?*

The discovery of oneself as a creative source, combined with the permission to create art can break the logjam of fear in a beginner artist. Those who witness the resulting deluge will be surprised by the changes in said person. This is true for everyone at the start of any artistic practice, but it's doubly important for out-of-line artists to understand their internal resources because they will need to rely on them a lot in their small place. It's not unlike coming out; the permission to be oneself is much the same. Of course, sometimes the two actions – coming out as an artmaker and coming out as LGBTQ, or as a mental health consumer/survivor, or an assault survivor, or an addict, or any combination of these – can happen close to one another in time. Permission works that way. That said, it is also true that there are many people who live private lives while being public artists, and we should not assume that artistic reve-lation scorches everyone with the blinding light of truth. But telling the radical truth is addictive. You may grow dissatisfied with half-truths. Change itself may be soundless, but when you switch to telling your truth more often, it's practically guaranteed that people will sound off about the changes they see in you. So you need to find your people.

*

Warning: your people – your artistic peers, mentors and comrades who will strengthen and inspire you, or at the very least offer tangi-ble proof that what you do is a force in the world because they are working on it, as well – will probably not appear exactly as you pic-tured. They may not appear cool, so go easy on them, eh? You will find them by looking at what they produce rather than what they look like. Your number one job as a developing artist conducting your own inquiry into the art world you want to create is to search out art in your vicinity, and that means being attuned to the po-tential of the work. Is no one in your community writing the songs you want to write? Fair enough, but then your next task is to find a musician in your community and ask them how they learned to play, sing, conduct, compose. It does not matter if they do not write music that you like. They are – by the simple act of being practicing musicians – storehouses of knowledge about that world. Ask them what to read, listen to, where to go to school, who to emulate, how. Ask them what they are writing and listen to it, sincerely. Give their art your attention. Most importantly, discover how "hidden" artists in your world found the strength to be artists in an artless or per-haps even hostile community. This is good information, and will be vital to you as you make your choices and build your cohort.

Another thing to remember is that your relationship to money will always shape how you look at the world. It is not as though people don't change, or, as it is popular to say, "reinvent themselves"; sure we can, as far as appearances or experiences goes. These appearances and experiences might make up 99 per cent of what people know about you and what you know about others. However, earning a steady paycheque will not make you 100 per cent relaxed about your bank account if you have grown up in a low-income context, just as having a book published will not necessarily make you 100 per cent confident in your artistic ability. One of my students reading David Sedaris's *Theft By Finding* declared, "Why is he so down on himself? He's a published author!" Why indeed? Some things about growing up in the striving class – the class that has left the social and material starvation of the working class and is moving anxiously toward being middle class – never go away, and this is not necessarily a bad thing. An outsider perspective is a good platform for anyone who wants to make art. Who better to offer different views, to change structures or to address different material than someone from (and still on) the outside? Who knows better what makes – and unmakes – a life than those of us who have lived or still live outside some of the structures of privilege?

In my world of teaching and writing, we talk about structural privilege a lot, but that might not be true for you. So here are some definitions: *privilege* is a term used to refer to the condition of belonging to social positions of relative power via advantages bestowed by circumstances of birth, or sometimes via effort that is relatively distant and historically positioned, like the class mobility that many white North Americans experienced after the Second World War. Through those dynamics of belonging, such advantages give people relatively easy (or "privileged") access to the benefits of mainstream culture and institutions. People are variously privileged, and while economic power is a primary marker of privilege, economic advantage and opportunities to gain such are often affected by race, gender identification, sexuality, class, region, education, mobility and other factors. Some people are granted important opportunities (including the chance to mess up without punishment), and their privilege normalizes this; others with less privilege are denied those same "normal" opportunities on the unspoken and sometimes unconscious basis that they are suspect and must prove themselves worthy. That's a problem. It becomes even more of a problem when it is not acknowledged as built-in structural inequity by those with privilege.

While it's true that a white working-class woman is not as privileged as a middle-to-upper-class white man, it must be said and acknowledged frequently that whiteness – in North America and Europe – comes with a free pass, which can be translated into all kinds of things. Perhaps most significantly, it gives one freedom from being heavily scrutinized, judged and acted against in schools, in banks, while driving, while walking, at work – in all places and at all times. Do white women have less privilege than white men? Yes, but white women also have more privilege than BIPOC folks, and acknowledging privilege means acknowledging that privilege has a spectrum. New Zealand graphic artist Toby Morris's viral cartoon for *The Wireless*, "On a Plate," provides an excellent illustration of the very practical and daily ways in which privilege works, as well as how the most commonly privileged (i.e., white people, men, upper or middle-class people) view their advantages as earned rather than given.

I write this as someone who has not always been perfect in such matters. I am exactly privileged enough that I can write that sentence. One of the problems in acknowledging privilege is that in doing so we must also acknowledge a lot of things that many people do not want to talk about in any form: racism, white supremacy, misogyny, violence against women and girls and non-binary folks, national histories of violence against Indigenous Peoples, religious intolerance, sexuality, gender identity and, yes, class. So if we refuse to talk about those things – and especially if we shame each other when we do talk about them – our discussions of privilege are doomed to go nowhere.

I am uncomfortably aware that discussions of class have been appropriated by the alt-right movement, and are being used to justify increased violence against women and non-binary people, against black people, against Indigenous people, against Muslim people and other groups. I say *increased* violence because the framework that props up such racism and xenophobia has never been completely dismantled in North America, with the governmental treatment of Indigenous Peoples being the primary and most enduring example of structural inequity. But when I write and talk about class privilege, I am not thinking about how I can leverage my own experience of structural inequity to take advantage of others, but rather how we might acknowledge some solidarities and work together. As bell hooks puts it in *Where We Stand: Class Matters*, when we come to class-consciousness, we can find our public voice without the fear of being class-shamed. When I note that some of my privilege is hard won, gained through risk and bonehead errors and pursuit of goals beyond my star, I don't want to invoke the all-white frontierist attitude of "bootstrapping." A bootstrapping argument reinforces the lie that everyone who is willing to work hard has the same opportunities, and is a basic tenet of white supremacy. At the same time, I don't want to deny that working-class people of all races and genders work themselves ill – and sometimes to death.

The unspoken shape of privilege – and the accompanying fear of social humiliation – is behind one of the most consistent questions I hear from beginner writers: Who will be allowed in the literary world? As in, will they be *allowed* to write, because so much has already been indicated to those like my students that art is for "other" people. And what about subject matter? What is allowable? I've answered this question many times, and can see that many people don't believe me at my first or even second answer. The dialogue usually goes something like this:

Students: What topics are we allowed to write about?

Me: Anything. The most appropriate subject for art is anything that has happened or could happen or could be imagined by a human being. Or an alien. Or an animal.

Students: No, really.

Me: Really.

Students: (Profound silence while they stare at me and think of subjects like sexual violence and racism and gender identity and the death of their best friend in high school and more racism and different violence and the growing silence that is extremely loud.)

Me: *Anything.* I won't grade you on your choice of subject matter, but rather on your use of technique and form. Let's read this story by Ivan Coyote or Jorge Luis Borges (or this essay by Taiaiake Alfred or Dorothy Allison, or this poem by Wayde Compton or Sachiko Murakami) and maybe that will give you a better idea of what I mean.

For each group I teach, there is always one text that busts open the issue of subject matter, and I never know what that text is going to be. For example, once it was Natalie Diaz's pantoum "My Brother at 3 a.m.," a poem that shows that addiction, mental illness and all the ways of families talking and not talking about those things are good subjects for a poem – and also that writers can, as Diaz does, write about seemingly uncontrollable subjects in a traditional form. A poem like "My Brother at 3 a.m." ushers in an important moment in a writing class. At the start, beginner writers cannot believe that they will be allowed to write about the subjects and events that have shaped their lives, despite the fact that almost all of them have been attracted to art for such possibilities, stated or implied. At the start,

I say, "yes, you can write about that" repeatedly, while students say, "no, couldn't be" over and over. It's the moment when I see the hugeness of the limitations that we place on people's lives, here in the twenty-first century. It's the moment when beginner writers might see that it need not always be so. They are stranded in a forest; meanwhile I am standing in front of them in a field, and Natalie Diaz, Terrance Hayes, Kristiana Kahakauwila and Marilyn Dumont are all there with me, waving. We are saying that the field is theirs to roam through. The beginner writers, though, are still in the forest, saying that they'd love to enter the field but they can't trust that they will not be attacked for stepping into it. That's usually when I talk about class, privilege and the need for solidarity. Beginner writers, on hearing from each other that they are not alone, begin to listen to each other and slowly venture out into the field, dropping their explorations on my desk at the end of class.

I also note that sometimes people arrive in my class because they are looking for ways to dodge the limitations that have been placed on them. Sometimes, people are "allowed" (by parents, by cultural expectations, by their peers) to make art under certain circumstances but not others. You can sing, but only in the church choir. You can join a taiko group, but can't drum for a rock band. You can write genre fiction, but don't even think of going to a poetry reading. Sometimes people show up in my classes hoping and intuiting that these restrictions can be circumvented.

A life of artmaking pretty much shreds such constraints. But there is work involved. When my former student Ashley Hommel-Hynd won the 2017 Pacific Spirit Poetry Prize, she thanked her grandmother "for all her difficult choices, the life she led and the life she hid, and the cheekbones she gave my body." Ashley also thanked Professor Jenny Kerber, in whose class Ashley started to think that she would be allowed to write about her Indigenous heritage, and me, in whose class she drafted the poem "First

Communion (1992)." When I saw the poem in draft, I felt its great abrogative power: how it challenged me to admit a lack of understanding, my whiteness, my prairieness. In my head I heard what Métis poet Gregory Scofield told me when I interviewed him in 2006: "When I'm writing poetry, it's a very solitary thing – it's just me and the Grandmothers, the Grandfathers, the history." A teacher should know when to shut up and move aside. I said, "Keep going. You know what you're doing," and got out of the way. I moved aside, and Ashley moved forward. She had cracked open the constraints of subject matter, form and language, and all I could do at that point was cheer.

*

Flexibility and adaptation are good watchwords to live by if you are the least bit out of line. Artists are adept at finding their art – and reasons to practice their art – everywhere. Part of your art is finding out where it lives in the world, even and especially where it lives in your small and sometimes stifling home place – what Richard Hugo calls "the triggering town" in his book of the same name. Hugo divides mid-century American poets into "insiders" and "outsiders," and notes that "knowing can be a limiting thing."

And sometimes knowing can be a scary thing, too. The Mennonite-Canadian poet Di Brandt, in her 1996 essay collection, *Dancing Naked: Narrative Strategies for Writing Across Centuries* (and elsewhere), wrote extensively about how becoming a writer was the most shocking thing she could have done in the eyes of her birth family, that her mother was "paralyzed with fear by the event of her daughter's becoming a published writer." Other writers postpone their artistic development until they're a bit older and have more control over their futures, but sometimes family and age and riskiness have less to do with our postponement of an artistic practice than the ability to earn money to support ourselves. When I asked Brenda Schmidt, who grew up on a farm and is a skilled nature photographer as well as a fantastic writer, about this need to balance practical demands with artmaking, she wrote about the juxtaposition between family creativity and its uses:

> My dad is highly creative, could fix anything, and invented lots of things for the farm and for fun. My mom was also a genius when it came to making clothes, curtains, bedspreads and whatnot. Money was hard to come by; no end of imagination and creativity kept the farm going. . . . I could not afford a BA until well into my career as a nurse. My career choice was pragmatic and made by me. I wanted to be able to support myself and I did not want to be poor ever again. I knew nursing would keep a roof over my head.

My early training as an actor mitigated the scandal of my becoming a writer. Being an actor for the handful of years I did it professionally has had the benefit of making being a writer look like a stable and sober career choice. It also taught me early about public rejection and artistic practice, and a lot about the Great Ravenous Furnace of Ego – my own, most of all. Arts communities can be fun and lively and great places to find people who accept your vision of artmaking, but an out-of-control ego that loves their little bit of power can ruin the experience. Every artist needs to know how to say – aloud or to themselves – that the senior artist does not know everything. This is admittedly harder for women, who are socialized toward a highly negotiated professional niceness, than it is for men, who, in North America, have social practice in an aggressive culture of jockeying for position, and who will be admired and often rewarded for protecting their ideas. It is also harder for BIPOC artists of all genders, speaking against the whiteness of hiring or curatorial practices. But all of us can know our own minds, and talk with our people, our artistic cohort.

＊

And where do I find my people? One of the most enlivening aspects
of an artistic community is the scope and range of skills that people
have. Any writers group will contain visual artists, a fact I discover
each year when I ask students for volunteers to design the poster
for our year-end reading. Any dance troupe contains actors. The
cast of every play contains at least one musician. Any choir contains
people who can play multiple instruments, as well as songwriters,
poets, actors and comedians, because no art exists in isolation, and
art is contagious: once you immerse yourself in one art, you will
find yourself very susceptible to the possibilities of another med-
ium. Painters and musicians often show up in my writing courses
because they have twigged onto a need for words – the right words
– in their primary artistic practice, and want to try writing poetry
to enhance what they can do in their chosen field.

One art leads to another, and finding an art that is practiced
deeply and widely in a community can yield all kinds of benefits
to your artistic development. When I asked my (mostly writerly)
colleagues about their artistic development, they responded with
a wide swath of talents: visual art, photography, sewing and knit-
ting, painting and performance. I loved, too, that so many pointed
out that while it is great to be paid for your art, the training that
comes from community art is invaluable as instruction for how
to live in the world. Canisia Lubrin, author of *Voodoo Hypothesis*,
points out that community art cannot be confined to or defined
by a pay category: "I don't recall anyone ever putting a price on
art. I think it was likely due to the history of the uses of art in
Black liberation and agency. Expertise was never defined. It was
embodied. Self-evident in a commitment to art and its practice."
Lubrin credits her grandmother's storytelling and her own childhood experience of performing in school and community theatre

as formative artistic experiences. Her description of participating in the sewenal on St. Lucia is a great example of the power – and possibilities – of community performance:

> What was most dynamic were the freestyles, the impromptu lyrics that were conjured from whatever home the sewenal happened to be in at the moment. Those songs were laid over familiar folk rhythms: drums, fiddles, shak shaks. Always, the point was humour and wordplay. Complete and unapologetic laughter. And sometimes the lyrics stung, when they cut into the autobiographical, things people would rather others not know (gossip)/narratives they'd wish to control. But the community nature of a thing like the sewenal meant that no one was immune to this; it was part of the thrill and social contract, loved as much as it was dreaded by *everyone* – regardless of class. The prime minister was not exempt. You dreaded that everyone would be listening in because the valley knows how to amplify sound. You knew that those nearby would be in your yard before you'd had a chance to offer drinks to the performers. I learned a lot about rhythm, sound, meter and narrative urgency that way. I also learned about the social and public dynamism and responsibility of art creators and the complexity of their relationship to audience.

I really like Canisia's note that the communal performance of the sewenal was both loved and dreaded, and that no one was hidden from its far-seeing eye. My own experience with community performance showed me how much people learn not because they are comfortable, but specifically because they are not. People learn because the situation demands it. I used to sing with a choir and several times wrote comedic interstitial pieces for performance between songs, and other choir members stepped up to perform them when I asked for volunteers. Sometimes I wrote nothing at all but still chose two people to perform between songs and said to them, "Find a way to get us from one song to another; maybe use that story you told me last week during coffee break," and left them to it. Once, a choir member panicked and said, "Aren't you going to write something for us? I'd feel better with a script!" But I knew they could do it without me putting words in their mouths, and said so. The piece they came up with – a gently humorous banter on sexuality, belonging and otherness – was something that I couldn't have written. It was entirely their own, and was warmly received in every performance. My part was to be a writer with faith in other writers: to pen nothing but allow them to write. And they did.

So we find our people in part through research, in part by daring to show up and call ourselves beginner artists, and in part by mutual agreement to regard each other as artists. It can feel like a mass hallucination at first, but you will prove it to be real soon enough. I can't stress strongly enough the role of generosity in this catalytic experience. Many artistic communities form by happenstance and luck, and that is perfectly fine: writers groups, casts of plays, choirs, bands, classes, workshops, readings, special events. Be generous to each other when this happens. Opt for more variety and inclusion rather than less. When a spirit of generosity is not present, things get bad quickly, and it is worse than an individual's feelings getting hurt, though that happens too, and can be awful to witness. The leader, instructor or senior artist must model generosity for the less experienced artists in the room. For instance, a literary reading that includes everyone from beginners to writers with multiple books is a great lineup. For beginner artists, for people who have come to art at every stage of life, performing on the same bill as a senior writer is a heady experience. It is just as important for the seasoned writers to hear beginners. The senior artists, if we are listening or at all present, will be reinspired by the beginner writers and see that our

work has done something, has fostered permission or an environment or something that has filtered down, even thousands of miles
distant and/or several years later, to somebody.

*

Let's say, for the sake of discussion, that you have looked around
your community and been successful in finding one of "your people": that is, someone who is doing it, living the artist's life, or at
least living it more than you have been.

For now, as you are discovering this person, you are just watching to see what happens. Because it feels as though anything could.
Maybe you are staring. Maybe you are watching them more surrep-
titiously in the manner that you've been taught, a little suspicious
(also in the manner you've been taught), because *come on*: Who
does this person think they are, swanning about like they are interesting and artistic and special? Maybe you resent this person. Envy
will do that. Do you find yourself crossing your arms in a huff and
questioning their right to make art? Why do they get to sing the
solo, wear a feather boa, read their poetry in public, paint in bold
triangles; how are they getting away with it? Why do others just accept
them? What do they have that you don't? If, like me, you grew up
in atmospheres where we were told to "be ourselves," but were also
carefully taught that "ourselves" had to line up with stifling standards, and furthermore that we, too, must carefully teach others
not to transgress, then this is a boatload of stuff to buck against.

What they have – that person swanning about, hitting the high
note; that person with the hot poems wearing a belted choir robe
and pointed boots as street clothes; that person you envy and wish
to emulate despite yourself – is very important and enviable. They
have permission. Someone gave them licence to swim against the
tide as themselves. Someone said to them that it was not only their
privilege to do so, but more, it was their duty, their life's work. By

being in the beginner artist's world, by flaunting their style and passions, by daring to be, someone gave that beginner artist permission. The second important thing about permission is that the beginner artist needs to recognize the licence that this grants, and that takes courage.

This usually doesn't happen in a flash, though it might. If you grew up in a community where art is "for other people," it may happen more slowly. It happens one piece at a time. It can seem like it's taking forever.

Sometimes, when you are hacking your way through the undergrowth toward an out-of-line life, you might have no other plan than to keep going. This is perfectly okay. Do it enough and you will start to recognize your chances, or at least recognize someone else who has taken those chances and listen to them. It is possible that I owe my writing career to Tom Chan, my grade eight English teacher, who paced back and forth at the front of the classroom in a three-piece cream-coloured suit and was wildly passionate about writing; who would put on a piece of music and get us to freewrite; who directed us in a Reader's Theatre performance of Stephen Leacock's *Behind the Beyond* and never once said that we didn't understand the material, which we manifestly did not. He also put together creative collection shows where we read our own writing accompanied by slides and music that he had compiled.

I think of the work that Mr. Chan put into those performances, in a junior high school in Winnipeg in the 1970s, where sports were the currency and art was decidedly not, how he insisted with his lessons and his actions that our writing and our speaking were audience-worthy, and it makes me a little wobbly. He revitalized the school newspaper and made sure that we were all published in it. He was also a new faculty member and an ethnic minority in the 1970s in a small prairie city. Okay, that's done it; now I am dizzy with his daring and his love for us, all of us distrustful teens at the most awkward age. Much has been said recently about safe spaces in the classroom, and much has been misconstrued in these conversations, comparing safety to coddling. But a safe space to create, whether the beginner artist is fourteen or seventy-four, is about creating a cushion on which people can land, so that they can take risks. Many of us were taught that risks were not for people like us. A safe learning space is not a cocoon. It is a rope on which climbers are belayed; it is a spotting partner when you are trying to lift more weight.

*

But what if, for example, you establish a creative writing group in high school so you can talk to other writers about your sci-fi novel set on a planet without gender, and half the people who show up want to write moody nature poetry? Or vice versa, where you're the poet and you are surrounded by people who say that only fiction is real writing and poetry is just emotion-filled pap? Shout-out to my colleagues on the student literary magazine *Off the Cuff*, in Kelvin High School, who, when we were in grade eleven, sat in a circle for an hour one Wednesday and said of every single poem in the pile: "Too emotional." I argued that those poems should go into the magazine, and thanks to teachers Karen Collin and Muriel Jamieson, who oversaw our argument, they did. What if you join a community theatre group because you love Tomson Highway's plays, but the group asks you to play Biff in *Death of a Salesman*? What happens if your influences, and your vision, are infinitely cooler than the other beginner artists with whom you are surrounded? You look around and think, "These people are okay, but they are not really my people. I still feel alone and misunderstood."

This happens. It happens all the time. Bottom line, you are right: these may not be "your people" in the largest sense of the world, but what's stopping you from being with them for a little while? You never know when the intersections between people, genres, styles and techniques, between one community and another, will meet and strengthen your art. This doesn't mean letting go of your vision, but it can mean trusting that your art is yours and it's always going to be there. You can leave it for ten minutes, for an hour, for a week to go explore someone else's ideas, then return to your own practice refreshed and stimulated and ready to create something new for yourself. You might even lead the group in another direction. People can't put on Highway's plays if they've never read him. Sometimes you need to lend them your copy of *The Rez Sisters*.

Sometimes you've got to work with what's in front of you. How can you work with what other people offer you and adapt it to your own artistic practice? Fiction writers find their prose gets stronger after they study poetry. Painters find the study of music changes how they see. Working with whatever (and whomever) is in front of you sharpens your own skills at articulation. Want to strengthen your own vision? Try explaining it to someone else. Want to extend your vision? Try collaborating with another artist's practice. Sometimes – and maybe sooner than you expected – you will be the confident one, and others will be newer to the practice or more hesitant than you. You have to be brave to be generous, to pay attention to someone's work when you don't see yourself in it. Have faith that your generosity will create a more forgiving world, a bigger practice, more possibilities in a small place.

If it's brave to be generous, it's also brave to take leadership without squashing people. Sometimes that means bringing someone else into your protective circle. Be the one who grants permission. I can still remember C, from a very early workshop I took, and the way she spent a lot of time writing feedback on one of my poems. The poem, for the record, was not very good, though it did represent the extent of my abilities at the time, and I had worked hard on it. C gave me the generous gift of attention, for she was far and away the best writer in the room, and I was blown away that she spent so much time on my poem. I saved that copy of the poem for years – the one she wrote all over – and read it whenever I felt like I was going nowhere fast. I thanked her for it at the time, but she left the workshop a few weeks later and I never saw her again, and now I think that I didn't thank her enough.

If you have been mocked for your artistic tendencies, you might feel protective of your projects and goals. You might feel defensive, or even aggressive. I have been in groups in the theatre, music and writing worlds where fragile people have isolated themselves from the group through aggression. Often they declared themselves to be the only one there who was true to the art: the only one with talent or drive, the lonely and brittle "best." It's painful to watch, because this may be a person with considerable ability who is hampered by their fear of being in a group of many talented people. Early in my artistic life, I was in a group with a young man who was much-lauded in his small community, who told us that we should get ready to give up our careers in despair because he was about to "knock us all on our asses" with his awesomeness. A senior group member suggested, gently, that everyone was there to practice their own art, that an audience was not to be abused or held in contempt but was rather something to cultivate. The senior artist's advice was excellent, especially when the audience is made of your peers. Aim to contribute to their practice, not to best them.

Young artists can be competitive. Maybe you come from a small community in which you are the "only artist," known in your high school or community as *the* poet, singer, girl who can draw, guy who can dance. Transitioning to having artistic friends and collaborators can be a big adjustment, and sometimes, after the heady thrill of finding others like you, you may be shocked to discover that others are better at a specific artistic practice than you currently are. The good news is that if you are brave and observant, you will see that there is room for everyone's art, that the world's appetite for art is not predicated on a capitalist system of scarcity, but rather, sustained by our own capacity for creativity.

To illustrate: a good friend moved to a rural town and decided to run some poetry readings, inviting poet friends as guests and advertising the events to the town. He was smart and brave enough to put up posters all over town, to discuss it at his workplace the next town over and to chat about the event to anybody who asked, assuring them that they didn't need to do anything special – just show up and listen. The readings attracted thirty people each, filling the small space in the café and creating a good audience for the poets, who sold books, and for the café owners, who sold food and drink and some local art that was available for purchase. This town was ready for art, and my friend's talent was being brave enough to show his love for the written word and generous enough with his time to make it happen. Art is very accommodating; it will happen wherever we let it.

Every artist, at some time or another, will be too edgy, too much, too radical for their surroundings. This can happen often; it can become a way of life if you are significantly out of line. Remember to find allies, to be generous rather than afraid. Remember that hidden artists can be unpredictably good. Sometimes the confident people share their good work, and then the most socially awkward person feels emboldened by that to pick up a guitar, at which point you discover that they have been teaching themselves for the last year and have told no one.

Be generous. You never know to whom you'll be giving permission.

*

When I was about sixteen, I said to the only professional writer I knew that I had been doing some thinking about writing, and he laughed.

I was crushed. It took me a few years to figure out that he wasn't laughing at me so much as at everyone in the world who asked him for writing advice but never actually wrote anything. Perhaps he was also laughing at himself for his own writing habits. Because what you've written, how recently, how much, how well and when you'll be seeing your work in print is an obsession for most writers. I include myself in this.

But what I was saying to him – because he asked – was that I had been writing and therefore had some thoughts about writing that I wanted to discuss with him; he thought I was saying that thinking about writing was writing. I was only sixteen and already didn't believe that. From this distance, it's hard for me to say whether his disbelief, his cynicism, his bitter laughter was about gender, age or class, or perhaps all three. But when you are a beginner artist – whether you have actually made art or are thinking about how to do it – it's important to find someone who takes you seriously. Don't feel too sorry for me, because despite this story I did find those people: teachers and the parents of friends and older artists that I encountered, by hook or by crook, because I craved such contact.

I confess to having a deep and abiding love of stories about how people met the mentors who got them to take those first few important steps. In John Leguizamo's graphic novel bio, *Ghetto Klown*, his first acting coach is depicted as a little wizened old woman living in her apartment in Brooklyn and taking absolutely no shit from the young, motor-mouthed Leguizamo. She was not edgy or cool, but she made him work, and he got acting jobs. Don't judge a mentor by their cover. People who will take you seriously as an artist may not look especially cool to you or to the outside world. Be assured that they are undeniably and indefinably awesome, but stuck in your small town or conservative community or class-bound suburb. Remember that their exterior may be a consciously chosen camouflage, or they might wear a social uniform for their job, or they may know that which takes years to find out: that the time and money spent on looking artsy is far better spent on making art, sharing it and talking about it.

For me, these people include: my grade eight English teacher, my grade seven math teacher, my supervising teacher on the high school newspaper, my long-suffering even-tempered drama teacher for three years of high school, my friend's painter mother, my engineer next-door neighbour, my dad's best friend who could play nearly anything on the piano and ukulele by ear and always encouraged me to sing, my minister from ages seventeen to twenty-five who had read everything and was willing to talk about books any time, the director in the first play I did outside of school and the older actors with whom I shared the stage and who just nodded when I tried to act and was bad. These people were, in no particular order: snaggle-toothed, dressed perpetually in brown, elderly with ears that stuck out, devoted to suits that were too tight, overweight, plagued by a fright-wig hairstyle, too old, too suburban and judged unlovely by the world in a thousand different ways. Most of them weren't "good-looking" people and neither was I. For me, read also: snaggle-toothed, pale, with awful hair, wearing clothes that did not fit and stuttering. None of this mattered to my mentors or to me as a budding artist, but I mention it because in our selfie-driven lives, physical beauty has taken on an impossible-to-match prominence. If we are looking for gorgeous mentors, we'll never find them. If we are waiting for the right "artistic look," we will never get anything done.

A student I had never met came to my office once and asked if there were any published poets teaching courses. I said I taught a poetry writing course that would run the next term. He said, "No, real poets who have published." I said, "Yes, that's me," and pulled my three books down from the shelves to show him. I wasn't insulted; sometimes people need to see physical evidence. He examined the books carefully. Maybe I had changed my name to this poet's name to fool students? Then he said, "No, I mean – someone else. Someone ... younger." Now, I have two colleagues who are a bit younger, but they both teach fiction; I'm the only poet in the department. "Ah," I said, "you are out of luck there: there's just me." I would, if I could, wish everyone a world of fantastic choices, but the truth is sometimes when you are starting out, there's just me or someone like me. It may relieve you to know your job as a student is not to emulate me but rather to use me as a ladder: climb my rungs.

There is another theory, not so well formed, and about which I have mixed feelings. It's that people need negative forces to push back against. I am tempted to skip this subject, but since so many of us encounter naysayers, it is best to address them. If you feel like it's too early in your exploration to read this right now, skip this piece and come back later. It will still be here when you need it.

There are mere jeerers and there are people who will provide you with useful grit. There are also dangerous people, and they are a different subject altogether. It can be hard to tell the difference.

I was once enrolled in a workshop with ten other people, and some of the writers went out for a drink after the evening workshop. I didn't go with them so I don't know what happened that night, but when we met the following week, a shift of major proportions had occurred. A few participants decided that they were the only real writers in the group and they lost no time in making their attitude known to the rest of us. I was a bit surprised, especially since I had known one of these writers for more than a year and would have testified that he was a real mensch. But he was puffing himself up and scoffing at others, claiming that he and two other male writers in the group had "higher standards." If I am generous, I could say that they genuinely believed that their demands would force us all to toughen up and be better poets. But I live in the real world, and so I will say that they acted like misogynist jerks. Well intentioned or not, their plan might have worked better had their poetry been appreciably better than what the rest of us were writing, but it was not. If you set yourself up as superior, it had better be true if you want to prove anything. As it was, I laughed out loud one night when one of them gave feedback on my poem with this opening salvo: "This is actually good. I'd say it's almost as good as my poem. You're getting there." I hooted – an unsophisticated, small-town expostulation of incredulity – and said, "Oh yeah, ya think? Almost as good as your poem?" He nodded soberly and said, "Almost." Game on.

What followed was weeks of gender essentialism in which poetry was touted as a male space that women could not really occupy because women couldn't write about "real things." The women of the workshop pushed back, citing Virginia Woolf, Anna Akhmatova, Maya Angelou, Joy Harjo, Adrienne Rich, Marge Piercy and Louise Glück. The men made dismissive gestures like they were waving away mosquitoes; it turned out that by "real things," the men had meant "violence," which was creepy. Undeterred, we brought in poems to refute them, each of which were refused as not being up to their rigorous standards. The night it came to a head, one of the other women brought in Emily Dickinson's "My Life had stood – a Loaded Gun," and they rolled their eyes.

I stayed with the workshop, kept writing and took nothing they said seriously for the weeks that were left. Other female poets left the group because they felt so summarily judged by the male students. Not one of us had published a damn thing at that point. I could hardly blame the other women writers for leaving, and I'm still not sure why I stayed. The well of literary fellowship was poisoned. The bastards had the gall to look pleased with themselves. I never knew what the best poet among us – a thoughtful and well-read older man – thought of what was going on. He looked askance at the younger men but said nothing. Perhaps by then he had seen it all come and go. He didn't look enlivened by the discussion; he looked embarrassed. When the next year came, I found a different workshop – an advantage of being in a big city meant there were lots to choose from – and I never saw those guys again.

What bothers me about it all these years later is that it was so needless. It served no purpose at all but the stroking of their egos. They ruined the group because they had decided arbitrarily that their poems were better. I entered my first workshop with a chip on my shoulder; I have been judgey in the past and can't deny it. But there's a difference between what a terrified beginner adopts as a form of self-protection and the kind of targeted attacks made against others because of gender, race, age or class. This was bullying by adult men who should have outgrown such tactics. Maybe it arose from insecurity, but I have long since ceased to care about its source. This was the first time I'd seen this in action in a literary community, and it would not be the last. I have seen divisions that appear more subtle but can be just as vexing when participants divide by education or social class, by style and by age.

Aside from bullies, you might also run into grit-suppliers with actual content: a teacher who urges you to write differently, or a friend who doesn't get your writing but asks smart questions that you had not yet articulated. This is good information, though it may feel like a poke in the eye. A teacher who wants you to write differently may be right or wrong about what a piece needs, but they will invite you into a conversation and *voila* – you are talking about your writing. The teacher may also get you to articulate your aims in order to defend them. Depending on how good a writer – and how skilful a teacher – your instructor is, they may also provide you with information on how to take the next step, how to go further in your project, how to solve a problem, how to change your piece for the better. It's good to remember that what is offered as criticism is sometimes ego, masked by a veneer of certainty. A real critic has real evidence. Don't be afraid to ask for it.

A student came to my office one day to complain: he hated coming to class but he really wanted a mentor. "How can I find a mentor?" he asked. I defined a mentor for him as someone with whom he would have a kind of meeting of the minds, and that, though he and his (future, potential) mentor wouldn't always agree, the mentor would guide him toward becoming a better writer. He was very excited at this prospect, and said, "How can I get one of those?" It is a good question, and I have to say that I was also eager to have it answered, even though I was the one who was supposed to be answering it. The fact is that mentors are found through building relationships in a community, talking to people, attending workshops or classes, and discussing your work with senior artists. Some writing organizations have mentoring programs, but usually such programs are limited to twelve weeks or so.

Mentor has become a bit of a catch-all word: a verb/noun construct that is overused and often misapprehended. To wit: it is impossible to mentor a class of twenty to forty beginner writers. A class that size you can only teach. A writer with a full-time job can mentor a few writers for a few years. Mentoring is slow, personal, intense work. Teaching is, of necessity, faster, and at once more rule-bound and more expansive, encouraging a broad spectrum of exploration as a foundational study. Mentoring and teaching can both function to introduce beginner artists to community, and in the best-case scenario that can be awesome. I wish I could tell you that artistic communities are by definition heavens on earth, and that all artists are benevolent. Alas, no. Artists contain the same human frailties as everyone else, and sometimes have given themselves special licence to air those frailties to the detriment of others. While "others" includes just about everyone, it most especially includes beginner artists who are vulnerable to the machinations of power or just plain bad advice.

*

There is a scene in the film *All That Jazz* in which Roy Scheider's choreographer character sits down next to the crying, very pretty, but not very good dancer whom he has cast in his show (after having sex with her, of course, because this is Hollywood and the female artist is almost always an object rather than a subject). She who has not kept up with the rest of the (much better) dancers who were all cast for their abilities and professionalism; who has failed very publicly in rehearsal and whose failure makes it clear that she was cast not for her ability but because the choreographer was thinking through his pants. The choreographer sits down next to the not-very-good dancer, who is crying not just because she is humiliated and unskilled but also because everyone in the dance ensemble (and all of us in the audience) knows it. And he says to her, "I can't make you a great dancer. I don't even know if I can make you a good dancer. But, if you keep trying and don't quit, I know I can make you a better dancer. I'd like very much to do that. Stay?" She nods bravely.

He helps her up off the floor and they work and work and work (cue the montage), and then they work some more and by gum, he's a genius, because she *does* get better. She isn't as good a dancer as the woman beside her, but she is no longer screwing up; she listens and learns and she is no longer humiliated, no longer crying. She is dancing better than before. She blends in. She is part of the ensemble, and the narrative emphasizes that her lesson is learned, that he's a good teacher and that she's better than we all expected.

That screeching sound you hear is me yanking the needle off the record. That ripping sound is me tearing my hair out.

If I approach this same scene – and the set of beliefs it explores and promotes as creative pedagogy – from both the student's and instructor's point of view, it can be read differently. When this film came out, I was still a student. I would be a student in the tuition-paying sense for another five years, and a student in outlook for longer than that. At that time, this narrative made sense to me. I was an aspiring, intense, not ungifted person with big ideas and no experience. I liked the idea that when things fell apart, they could be patched up: that balance could be restored via her will and his talent. I liked that she was brave. I liked that he understood her humiliation and sought to assist her by offering her a future in the most realistic and pragmatic terms possible. I liked that, given her limited choices (learn or leave), she sucks it up and becomes not a great dancer, not a good dancer, but a better dancer.

What absolute misogynistic brainwashing that is. How dizzying it is to revisit this hogwash and remember how firmly I believed it.

Like so many naive young women with no protectors in the profession in which I worked, I was sold a bill of goods about artmaking – that I was supposed to be humble, to know my limitations, to be grateful for instruction and the attention of professional men, and to crave the chance to get "better" on the instructor's terms, as well as the chance to fit in enough that his indiscretion will go unnoticed (though in my example everyone in the dance company has noticed) because I (now that "better dancer") would then know enough, have my rough working-class edges smoothed away, and move in lockstep with everyone else.

In short, we were advised to work ourselves to the bone in order to be good enough to blend in, and to be, if we worked hard and were lucky, footnotes in the constructed narrative of a "great man."

One of the reasons that I have remembered this scene for so long, and even used it as a way forward, is because it is so reflective of my reality as a young artist. I was told over and over that I needed to take myself, and my art, seriously. I had no problem with this. In fact, coming from a background where no one thinks art can be made by people one knows turns out to be great training for taking yourself seriously: you have to, or you knuckle under to the status quo.

While I never expected non-artists to understand my drive, I was pretty taken aback to discover that plenty of older artists didn't take me seriously. I was not the prettiest girl on the planet, or even the prettiest girl in my cohort, but that didn't seem to matter. There were a lot of men who wanted to get a leg over, or at least practice the kind of flirty, cruel power play that was so popular at the time. (For "at the time," feel free to read "from time immemorial.") I even had one older performer tell me that I'd "never work in this town" if I didn't leave a party with him, and his admonition was so much out of a bad movie that I laughed. He got red in the face, and then there was yelling until an older actress stepped up and called him an idiot as she swept me away to a less-creepy part of the party.

That scene from *All That Jazz* – when the male director explains patiently to his latest conquest that he will use his genius to make her good enough to appear in his art – is head exploding, especially if you recall that she is only in said humiliating position in the first place because he wanted to get a leg over. This is not mentorship, although you'll meet plenty of people who will tell you that it is. I note that I was once naive to view this scenario as being separate from the sexual politics that shaped it. But the sexual politics lend the scene the dramatic flip to which we are accustomed in narrative, making us think that the choreographer, while a bit of a rat, is a "good guy" overall. After all, he didn't have to help her, right? And she became a better dancer in the end, didn't she? So it all worked out.

No.

Let's back up a bit. If I thought that the relationship between the choreographer and the dancer was not sexual, that he hired her with the intention of helping her improve, then maybe that would be the beginnings of mentorship. The mentoring artist – the director, choir master, choreographer, editor, instructor or senior writer

– has to coach the younger artist to make the art better for the sake of the art and not, as in *All That Jazz,* because he wants something from the mentee, be it sex or status or a crying towel. And definitely not because he is trying to hide his own mistake.

Let's give it the acid test: let's switch the genders and see what that gets us. The scene opens on a weeping young man (say Tobey Maguire, circa 1998) who is frustrated that he cannot get the dance steps right. Enter older female star and choreographer (say Beyoncé, circa now). She sees him slumped on the floor and sighs. He really was bad out there; he really can't dance. She regrets hiring him because she thought he was cute. But a deal's a deal. So, understanding that she could help his career, that she is the better, older, more sophisticated artist and that she knows what he does not, she hunkers down beside him, peers into his weeping face, and says, "I can't make you a great dancer. I can't even make you a good dancer. But I can make you a better dancer. Do you want to try?" He nods bravely. Cue montage in which she shouts at him and makes him practice over and over again as he falls or screws up, until finally he completes the turn and dances with the others without being noticed, and is super-grateful to her before vanishing from the narrative.

Maybe it's a failure of my imagination, but much as I want to picture that, I'm having trouble. Here's how I think this would work in the real world: she hunkers down beside him, peers into his weeping face and says, "I can't make you a great dancer. I can't even make you a good dancer. But I can make you a better dancer. Do you want to try?" He is incredibly insulted at this assessment. He stands up and threatens to tell everyone what a skank she is. No one gets away with humiliating him. "Fuck you," he snarls and stalks out. He goes on to audition for and gets a lead dance role in another company, and she eventually shows up at his dressing room, years later, crying, old, fat, broken down. He has his security men drag the sad old woman away. Does this sound familiar? I'm taking bets on which of these scenarios is more likely to appear on a screen near you ...

If you are a woman. If you are a gay man. If you are gender fluid in any way. If you are a person of colour. If you have a First Nations background. If you have a disability or any bodily "difference." If you are a straight guy who shows sensitivity or interest in art. If this is you – and this is most of us – you will encounter artist narratives that not only do not include you but are openly dangerous to you. If what my male friends are now telling me is true, this danger slimes its way even toward the most privileged of young white men. It is a function of the times that things have shifted just enough for them to tell me about being manipulated by the powerful when they were young actors. The patriarchy serves so few. I can think of many situations in which I, with members of my cohort, should have practiced better solidarity with the more vulnerable members of our group, but we didn't know that we could. That is not an excuse; that is our tragedy. If you make art, if you step out of line in any way, you will encounter real-world circumstances that will not just disappoint you, but can also damage you. I write this not to dissuade you, but to make you savvy. This is another excellent reason to have a cohort, a group of other artists to talk to. Individuals can be cut from the herd and isolated. Predators know this and proceed on exactly this basis. But groups can support their members; colleagues can practice solidarity.

So let's rewrite that *All That Jazz* scenario one more time, via the power of the cohort. In this version, the young dancer has not absorbed the idea that her value is sexual, but rather that her value is professional. When the choreographer suggests that he will offer her a part in the ensemble if/when she has sex when him, she walks out. She leaves the audition space and walks down the street to the café, where her dancer friends who also auditioned are waiting for her. One dancer friend has been outright offered a part in the ensemble based on her skill. Two have received callbacks. Three have received nothing. She tells them what the choreographer has said. Now everyone has a choice to make. Accept the job offer? Go to the callback? Take note and never audition for this choreographer again? Tell every dancer they know? None of these choices are easy, but they are worlds away from "I have no choice but to sleep with him to better my career."

I have used a fictional example here in part to move away from the various scandals that have rocked the literary and performing worlds in recent years. There are plenty, and the good news is that they have come to light as scandals about the abuse of power, rather than how they used to – as salacious gossip. People are beginning to name the misogyny that was once so accepted in the arts. I can't tell you what to do, and I don't want to simplify complex situations, but I can tell you this: you are already an artist. The most important lesson is to practice valuing yourself as one. There is always going to be someone with more power than you making decisions about how you are presented. These won't always be dangerous people, but the power of the cohort is yours. The more you are supported, the more you can take your time to choose.

*

There is a profound contradiction embedded in the writing life: what begins as a private pursuit – sometimes intensely private – necessarily becomes a public act, even long before publication, as beginner writers get more and more eyes and ears on their work. Most people are okay with half of this equation, loving either the private making or the public sharing, but the challenge for many of us becomes how to do both without losing our minds. A lot of shy people are artists, for good reason: creation is an endorsement and extension of their inner lives, a material manifestation of the world in which they spend a lot of time. It is evidence, for some, that they have existences beyond the too-loud, too-fast everyday world. The presentation of art work in public – at a book launch, in an art gallery or at a concert, even on stage as some performers are also introverts – is something to be negotiated (sometimes very carefully) in order to fulfil the social contract of the artist. On the other hand, a lot of gregarious people are artists, and the artistic challenges of the very public person are different: happy in a crowd, they have to fight against their gregariousness to carve out private space to think and make. The social person might also find themselves burdened with organizational duties in the community. If your skill is in glad-handing, talking people up, creating ease in a group, people are going to want you to do that all the time, sometimes to the detriment of your own work or health.

Most of us are somewhere in between. I have long understood that solitary time is necessary to my mental health, but when I took a position as a professor, the amount of time I needed to spend in public meant that I felt as though the job never left me alone. That was a class issue, as well, disguised (as it so often is) as a workload issue. It was not enough to work; I had to be seen working, obviously organizing and talking and contributing. It was also not enough to publish, to produce articles and books and poems; it had to seem effortless. It was not enough to achieve in one profession; I had to achieve in both. Hello, burnout: you bear a distinct resemblance to some bad advice I took once. I am by no means an anomaly in the arts. Outside the university as an institution, poet, songwriter and community organizer Janice Lee notes that she spends a lot of energy creating space for her art:

> My biggest obstacle is constantly advocating that art work is real work and ought to be paid and valued like all other work is under capitalism. In Canada, art work is not supported intrinsically through our cultural infrastructure. The most viable

way for me to make a living is to be an artist-entrepreneur who strings together one-time gigs non-stop, while also planning ahead and applying for grants to actually create new work. I am able to be a professional artist because I have the soft skills outside of artmaking, like grant writing, budgeting and business management to make it a financially viable career.

Janice's use of the word *non-stop* is resonant. I am often asked how I find time to write, and while I often do find the time, the truth is that no matter how much time I find, it never seems like enough. My sense of scarcity – a holdover from a childhood shaped by worry about scarcity – is always about time to write the books I have planned, and following my mother's death it has occurred to me that my stream of words, my infinite appetite for planning book projects and taking on writing tasks big and small is not infinite. This may seem obvious, but as someone who was always thinking of new projects, of what I would write as soon as I had the time, that fact, that this time is now limited, comes as a world-stopping revelation. I don't have special circumstances other than my age, but living parentless in the world has been enough to shock me into wondering why I believed in my own immortality for so long. That said, everyone has their own distracting formula for success over which they obsess. One of these is the book publishing deadline self-imposed by an author's concept of fame. I have heard many times from beginner writers that they must publish their book by the time they are twenty-five, or thirty, or thirty-five or else they will be ashamed for taking so long and be too old to publish. That is a fair enough belief in the moment; I would never discourage anyone from setting a personal deadline or from being ambitious. But remember that creating art is playing the Long Game; it will take your whole life to grow into the artist that you are. Being in a rush is a natural inclination, especially if your class upbringing emphasizes utility – that you must "make something of yourself," and do so quickly. Sometimes, parents or partners have allotted a time limit for the beginner artist to try out their artistic path, via a program of study or the completion of a project. Sometimes it's an agreement: *you can try being a full-time writer for two years and I'll support you, but then you have to start bringing in money.* So when I say that art is a Long Game, I mean that practice makes more practice because there is no perfect.

It's okay to stop for a while to take a job that pays. It's okay to stop for a while to refind your faith in yourself. It's okay to put a project on hold because you've reached the end of what you know for now. I keep hearing that art is fragile, but I disagree. Art is tough: it's we who are fragile. Art is not so delicate that you will lose it the minute you look away from it. Be warned that time goes fast, though, and having a strong practice will help you to begin again after some time away. I read those admonitions, that writers must on pain of humiliation write every day, and that their commitment to doing so equals their demonstrated commitment to their art. This is an indication of someone's privilege more than anything else. I love to write and do it whenever I can, but I don't have a life where it is possible to write every day, and I'll bet you don't either. I don't like how this admonition reinforces class distinctions and peer gloating. I don't like how sexist this is, how it finger-wags at young parents and other people living time- or energy-strapped lives and shuts them out of artistic conversation, or even self-definition as artists. Write every day? The advice to write on your lunch hour is great if you get a full hour for lunch, but not everyone does. The parent of young children (or the person working three jobs, or the person caring for elderly parents) barely had time for a shower. I don't like this classed culture of shaming people doing necessary work in the world over their lack of time to write.

*

Have lots of feelings? That is good material.
Have lots of questions? That is good material.
Have lots of observations? That is good material.
Have lots of weird ideas about how to do things with words? Good material.

The balance between public and private is elusive to many beginner artists, and the artistic community's interest in transforming private pain into salacious material – and better yet, to get the beginner artists to do it for them – is enormous and seemingly endless. The thrill of being allowed to write about taboo topics is undeniable: "What, I can write about sex and no one will tell me not to? Hey, this magazine will publish it? All right!" Fair enough, if that's your choice, but when taboo-breaking becomes a demand, young writers are pushed toward confessionality and overexposure by the not-always-objective demands of an editorial board who, for a variety of reasons, are hungry for sensation. I believe the same about the pressure to confess – however subtle – in assignments and workshops to impress peers and instructors with intense material. This is not a requirement for artmaking. Controlling the narrative means controlling when and if you allow private material onto the page.

Here are a number of outcomes that I have seen occur in beginner writers when they are pressured, overtly or covertly, to confess:

Shock: the writer writes what they didn't especially want to write, and feels trapped or manipulated by the insistence that it was required.

Shame: the writer refuses to write the private material and is shamed (overtly or covertly) for their refusal.

Isolation: the writer feels that if they don't write like the others, they will end up without a cohort, and they begin to widen the gap between themselves and other writers.

Envy: the writer begins to believe that their life is not as intriguingly beleaguered as everyone else's life, and they wonder if they are devoid of material.

Anger: the writer refuses to write dramatic material to satisfy others, which can turn into a simple refusal to write anything.

In matters of confessionality, to reapply F. Scott Fitzgerald's aphorism, the rich are different from you and me. They are different in their sins, as well: what could be a smart and sexy Park Avenue sin (as in the bestselling Judith Krantz novels of my youth) doesn't look smart or sound sexy on Tobacco Road, something Erskine Caldwell knew when he wrote the novel of the same name. Some of the cachet of confessionality is the shock of recognition: the feeling that someone has written something you knew about but about which you dared not speak. But if there's no shock of recognition, rather a classed eye roll and judgement ("*those* people, just what I expected"), then confession doesn't work the same way. I'm not saying that the working class or striving class shouldn't write confessional or quasi-autobiographical work; Jeannette Walls' *The Glass Castle* is a great example of a book that reveals the everyday life of a starving-class family. Jeanette Winterson's *Why Be Happy When You Could Be Normal?* is about poverty and blows the lid off of poetry as an elite practice. However, we should not pretend that confession will work the exact same way for all as it does in works written by the privileged who can confess to nearly anything and not face social judgement. Your context includes your class markers and, yes, people will judge. Write what you want, and be prepared not to be understood by all. That is part of playing the Long Game.

All the Feelings

My partner has told me the story many times of having an argument with his mother when he was fourteen: old enough to feel manly and independent, and still young enough to have no discernment about his behaviour and be grounded for it. He was late for dinner for a reason that he has since forgotten, but it led to an argument about his friends, or his activities, or his disrespect – even he has now forgotten that detail. But he remembers his anger and embarrassment at her scolding, and his crusty refusal to look at her, to hold onto his anger as righteous and masculine even as she served him the dinner he had missed because he was out somewhere breaking her rules. Like many women of that Greatest Generation, like my own mother, my mother-in-law had a sharp tongue and a deft hand in the kitchen, so apology or peacemaking often came in the form of food. He recalls eating his dinner that night, alone at the kitchen table because he had gotten in so late, long after everyone else in the family had eaten, and his mother arguing with and grounding him, then serving the food she had kept warm for him. He remembers thinking, as he ate the first few savoury forkfuls, "I hate you. I hate you so much. This is delicious." Love and anger swirled in him, returning him from the dark dramatic mountaintop of adolescent fury to his mother's kitchen. There he was loved, cared for, and there, infuriatingly for him and necessarily for her, that love and care meant keeping him within bounds for another few years. There was a sharp and powerful coexistence for each emotion within him. He felt love and anger, strongly and simultaneously, and not, as is often narrativized, with one feeling easing into the other.

I love this story for how it demonstrates the crash of emotions that we live with most of the time, the largely unspoken and rarely described tangle of emotion that shapes much of our inner lives but is so hard to name. This, for me, is at least part of the reason for art to exist in our lives, whether we are partaking of it or making it: because it captures and retains deep but necessary contradictions that slip away from our everyday use of language. Logic, with its compulsive need to categorize, will call something love and something else hate and shy away from complexity.

One of the rhetorical lies about language is its insistence that human beings experience emotions one at a time. I can't help but think of Elisabeth Kübler-Ross, who received so much public pushback after her study *On Death and Dying* was published in 1969, including her theory of "the five stages of grief": denial, anger, bargaining, depression and acceptance. People dealing with grief responded to Kübler-Ross that a nearer truth was that grief is potent because every emotion you can ever feel – including, potentially, joy and elation – gets sucked into its whirlpool. People can feel crazy with grief because sadness is the culturally and socially appropriate emotion, and they are instead feeling a dizzying mix of emotions that are culturally taboo to admit and admittedly strange to discuss. We're complicated, and when theories are proposed that simplify our experience, they annoy as many people as they relieve.

Map-making:
Your Time and Mine
Out of Line

Rainer Maria Rilke once wrote: "It is good for the rich and the lucky to stay quiet." I know my richness or luckiness is vast in some ways and slight in others. After twenty-five years of writing and publishing, I am rich in experience, and there's been luck involved, no question. Whether or not I was doing something right in my formative artistic years remains to be seen. But one thing is clear: I became a writer despite – or maybe because of – my un-writerly context.

With minor exceptions, few enough that I can count them on the fingers of one hand, every writer I know was a kid who didn't fit in, who lived in their heads as much as they could, dreaming of a world where they could show all of themselves, where they didn't have to crunch pieces of themselves down. Artists learn early how to dissemble; we grow up hiding in plain sight, sometimes reciting the party line until we can escape. Some artists never do escape their narrow, artless place, but have made their peace with it and set about making art anyway, somehow, someway.

For the record, no one has ever mistaken me for cool. I might have pulled off a cool half-second sometime in 1995, due to some momentary trick of the light, but I can't claim anything sustainable. I teach in a smallish university in the middle of farm country, where the culture drain to the Big City is a current against which I am always swimming. Many of my students come from very small places and view this city of 199,000 people as the big bad metropolis. I remember how it feels, to think that everyone else knows the scene and the language while you have to spend an enormous amount of energy on a daily basis just figuring out what is happening.

It's good to teach. Over the years I have encountered writers who hate to teach, and that's okay, too. The two skills – writing and teaching – do not necessarily go together. I didn't really know that I'd be any good at teaching back when I was one of those people who got a Bachelor of Arts degree thinking, "I can always teach." The word *always* in that sentence was meant to stand in for "never," the sentence itself performed as an usher for the non-conjoined but implied end-phrase of "if I screw up everything else." I was twenty-one and full of overweening confidence, as one ought to be at that age. I was not thinking of screwing up so badly that I would have to be (shudder) ordinary. My overweening confidence did not mean that I knew anything: I knew nearly nothing, was inheriting nothing, had no "contacts" or "background" in the profession I planned to take by storm, and was about to move hundreds of miles away from home, family and community to do it.

It may seem a fine distinction to say that I worried about not knowing things yet never really thought about failure, but such is the delicate balance of striving, of trying to become the thing no one you know understands. I had that feeling, of living mostly in my head, as a matter of survival when in the constant company of people who used the phrase *rich inner life* as an insult. I didn't think much about being ordinary because I felt surrounded by it. Do we think about air? Do fish think about water? The answer to both is that we do, when the air or the water becomes less than life sustaining, and so it was with me. Rebellion can happen in stages, or it can seem sudden when in fact it has been happening below the surface for months or years. I didn't think of failure because I thought in extremes: there was success and there was annihilation. "Failure" didn't loom in my mind as large as "hell." There was also the purgatory of "giving up" or "having doubts," and so I fell in with an intense and high-minded crowd of young artists who thought, much as I did, that such compromises were for losers, for those without toughness, talent, brilliance: that is, not for us.

All this makes me giddy with memory and with the nausea of being back in that either/or mindset. Talk about being set up to fail. It reminds me, too, of why it seemed so important to be exacting with myself. My parents and friends and neighbours were waiting for me to stop and come back and get married and get a job and have a baby and buy a house not too far from my parents – to "settle down." It's not entirely true that everyone wanted that for me, or that my family was so absolutely negative about my prospects, and the tiny pieces of encouragement I received were really important. I knew how to live on scraps. Suffice to say that if I had gone looking for someone to dissuade me from working to be an artist, I wouldn't have had to look far: about two feet away, at the members of my immediate family or my best friends in school. Nearly everyone I knew would have said, kindly and discouragingly, "Well, that was fun for a bit, but come on home. The library misses you."

I ignored people who argued for the ordinary because that was almost everyone I knew. It's also how I made myself brave enough to do the impossible: by thinking about what was waiting for me in that cramped space of compromise, the space of giving up, that space of being too afraid to go. I moved to the Big City and acted and wrote and published, and one day landed in an instructional job when a replacement instructor was needed. Through luck and by following the examples of smart friends, I figured out how to leap forward even when I was scared and I even leaped back to the home place to discover that it wasn't so small after all. It was down-right affordable to be an artist there. I noted this even as I moved away (again), and by the time I had tuned the machine that is my life to run on all cylinders – teaching, criticism, reviewing, writing, publishing and (oh yeah) love, which so far I've said nothing about – I was on faculty at a university in a city smaller than the one in which I grew up. On one hand, this had a kind of symmetry: not quite a full circle but maybe a wobbly ovoid. On the other hand, if I had been assigned the task of following that path, I would not have been able to see it. I teach to be able to afford to write, though I do love what I teach – from Canadian women's writing to dystopian novels to writing poetry and creative non-fiction. Many writers I admire do the same – Claudia Rankine and Larissa Lai and Marilyn Dumont and George Saunders and Kaveh Akbar. I worried for a while about settling but got over it; for me, writing well is the best cure for worry.

Yet my small city can seem far-flung on nights when exciting new writing is being launched a mere two-hour drive away. And the longer I live here, the more it is apparent to me that daring to be an artist outside the Big City is a kind of provocation that flies in the face of the common wisdom about moving to the big place and be-coming an artist. That's a good thing to do except not everyone can afford to live that way; not everyone has family circumstances that will support that course of action; not everyone wants to surrender to the pace of extremely urban life. There are all kinds of reasons for living "elsewhere," some of which apply to people practicing all kinds of art.

This is probably a good time to raise the spectre of envy: of the community of fabulousness that everyone expects to be there, welcoming them into the Big City; the influential circle of working artists and their moneyed friends who will introduce you to the right people and then fame, fortune and the endless adulation of millions. Making It. The Big Time. Success. This can happen, sort of, sometimes, after a fashion, with conditions. But it is mostly a function of the romantic imagination supported by the fact that every event curated on social media looks like "that" party, "that" launch, the one you could be at, the people you could be meeting, the book contracts you could be signing. It is also aided and abetted by the media's talk about "stars" of any arts scene. All you need to make art is yourself, some time and a sense of conviction, which is a bit like saying, "All you need to split an atom is an uranium isotope with an atomic weight of 235, a centrifuge and a little ambition." But there is a secret we keep from beginner artists: the best part is making art.

I don't want to pretend that I am never jealous of opportunities to hear great writers. I am, oh so often. But I've made my peace with being big in a small place, with the space I take up in a centre that is not a centre. Truth be told, no matter how much I pine for that fully imagined Technicolor life of seeing mind-blowing writers every night, I have to admit that when I lived in a big city, I couldn't always get to those events because work, because time, because I was living in a human body that needed rest and food and other mundane things. You know: real life.

Often, I look at the way power is spread across arts industries in Canada, and the closely writ methods of how to parse the who's who and what's happening and how to map out peer influences makes me a bit weary, if I'm honest. The cliché of "not what you know, but who you know" is at least a little bit true, and I don't want to assert from my place of relative knowledge that people don't make careers by finding great teachers or opportunities at the perfect time. Sure, that happens. But much more often, people build careers one move at a time: a chapbook of poems, a gig in a tiny venue where someone hears a song you wrote, a showing of your shoestring-budget film in a local theatre that leads to a festival invitation. Suddenly, things start happening, but such suddenness is years in the making and grows from practice and your own generosity. Specialized training programs can create instant cohorts, but within them, beginner artists are under pressure to immediately know and understand everything, and that pressure can be bewildering. Anyone who has spent a few decades pursuing their art will have colleagues and friends and helpful peers, and I'm no exception. But I developed my literary cohort when I was an adult with a full-time job, still full of questions but well able to make choices – even bad ones – about how I wanted to make stuff. It should also be said that the MFA program is a pretty incredible privilege on which not everyone can afford to spend the time or money. It can be hard to justify the expense to families. As poet Sylvia Symons writes, about enviously watching others take writing courses, "I went to university in the early '90s and in my mind, creative writing students were people who grew up with piano lessons and white-collar parents – possibly even tweed. (No racist jokes, no alcoholism, no violence.)" No kidding: it can seem like a magic formula, no matter how much someone like me says that you can get there from here. Or that, as Kurt Vonnegut Jr. wrote, "Writing...is a lot like inflating a blimp with a bicycle pump. Anyone can do it. All it takes is time." Well, time and effort. Time and effort and opportunity. Time and effort and the ability to recognize opportunity. And courage. Let's not forget courage.

*

A few years ago, a student came to my office. We were happily chatting about the course when he stopped and said, "I saw your book in the bookstore. And I bought it. And I read it." "Excellent," I grinned. It's good to be read. But that's not what he came to discuss. He looked at me sideways and finally said: "Okay, what's going on? You're a real writer. What are you doing here?"

He wasn't the first person to ask me that, and I'm fairly certain that he won't be the last. I see why it's an attractive myth, that real writers somehow live somewhere beyond: Paris or Greenwich Village or Harlem in the 1920s. But I know that this is a kind of writers' life that few people get to live. I used to believe in it fervently, and I'm not saying that this doesn't describe some writers' lives. The larger truth is more complicated, and I know that my student was struggling with his mental picture of a writer as it smacked up against the reality: unglamorous, everyday me, without elbow patches or a bestseller or a microphone or even a cup of coffee at my elbow, but with three books that displayed my name on the spine. He had also just had an experience that is head-spinning the first time you have it: he had read my book, spending a few hours with my subject matter, my stylistic choices, my voice, and to a certain extent in that slice of my brain, and now he was talking to me. That is very strange the first time you do it, and I remember vividly being tongue-tied by this effect when I was a beginner writer: the writer existed for me as private entity rattling around in my head, and then, bizarrely, as a public person who I met at a reading or book signing.

My star student, though, had more sang-froid than I did, and the question he asked is good. In fact, it's more than good. It's an essential discussion to have about writing, life and artistic practice as a material necessity. I am a professor of English literature and have been publishing poetry, fiction, research essays and creative non-fiction in Canada, the United States and the United Kingdom since 1992. I am always working on a manuscript, because that's what writers do, but I work in a university for three excellent reasons: 1) because universities value writers, though not always perfectly; 2) because I value my work with student writers; and 3) because I was not born to money and after a decade and a half of (barely) paying my bills via artmaking and cobbled-together jobs, I retrained as a scholar. It was a gamble that worked out for me, though it isn't a solution I would recommend for everyone, and it didn't answer my craving to make stuff. I love scholarly work, but I need the creative work, too. My dual-identity life isn't either/or for me, as it isn't for most artists: a lot of us need more than one intellectual or creative outlet.

But even so, I know that this is not the model of the artist that most people understand, so it's fair to feel a little puzzled by my dual identity. The ability to practice both these disciplines is a source of fascination for many, and I am often asked about it. I was a poet for many years before I was a professor, and for me there is no rigid dividing line between artist and teacher, between poet and professor, between teaching people to analyze texts and teaching writing. The metaphor of "wearing different hats" to do different tasks does not work for me; for my sanity, it is just one hat. I know dozens of people who do the same. Some of them mentored me and made this way of life imaginable for me. From them – and from considerable trial and error – I learned to bring my own creative practice into the classroom: art practitioner as professor, poet as instructor, working writer in the community.

But when I was an undergraduate student and beginner writer, I was taught that literature was written by people who didn't look like me, didn't speak like I did, didn't live where I did. (Yeah, didn't look like *me* – the striving-class white girl – so you can imagine what people from other backgrounds thought.) To give you a better picture, I grew up in a family that didn't know what an artist was. We didn't live under a rock, but we were working-class Scots in origin. None of us could read music, and the idea of playing an instrument was like travelling to the moon. None of us painted or drew, and none of us sang except off-key in church. We didn't go to galleries or museums, except on school trips. These things were not overtly disdained, but I knew that within my family these things were perceived as being "for other people." My parents weren't professors or intellectuals. They had both made it off the farm and out of the abject poverty that plagued their families during the Depression, and they counted that escape as their big success. The price they paid was the acquisition of a perpetually anxious view of the challenges they would face for defying the social order. They bought a house on the edge of the respectable section of the city and counted their blessings. They kept their heads down and paid the mortgage and mowed the lawn. They solved their infertility problem by adopting. They got and kept white-collar jobs and it seemed, if not the height of achievement, a kind of blessing that they would not disrespect by asking for more.

My mother was an inadvertent feminist role model because of her hidden disability. From the age of thirty-two, my mother bore a massive scar on her right leg – a four-inch by six-inch chunk of her shin removed down to the bone – which she hid by wearing pants 98 per cent of the time, and a floor-length skirt on rare occasions. This was during an era in which girls were not allowed to wear pants to school; this changed when I was in grade four, and was perhaps my first feminist protest when I joined small delegation of girls in petitioning the principal for the right to wear pants to school. My mother always wore pants; I didn't understand the necessity for me to wear a dress. My mother's missing chunk of flesh was the removal site of a malignant melanoma that she survived via early detection and several doses of an early form of chemotherapy based on the formula for mustard gas. There's a longer story there, but suffice to say that my parents had dodged war, poverty, infertility and cancer by the time they were thirty-four. They were, as that generation was, more adult by their twenties than I was in my forties. The knowledge that I had it easier than they did was rarely articulated, but it coloured everything.

But there were two things in my life that from an early age suggested that, despite my parents' admonition that to dream was greedy, there might be more to life. There was church, where readings from the Bible had a mysterious language that both embarrassed and intrigued me, and the library, where after getting a library card at the age of five, I took out as many books as possible every three weeks of my life. My father read. His taste wasn't literary, but it wasn't schlocky; he liked espionage and historical fiction. He taught me by example that a quiet hour with a book was the chance to pull your day in at the corners, to bring down a curtain on the world and rest within the lines of type. I had literary books arrive mysteriously in my room: Lewis Carroll's *Alice's Adventures in Wonderland* and Robert Louis Stevenson's *A Child's Garden of Verses*. Today, I am a bit aghast at these potent Victorian influences, but they were the books with which I was raised. I can still recite some of the poems from the Stevenson book. I also skated and played baseball, which was fine for a while, until my moderate talent at each was considered a liability. By the time I was fourteen, I had left athletics because I couldn't see the point in a system of worshipping athletes – usually boys I had known for years – as suddenly and unquestionably superior. This was another early feminist moment, and a class-based lesson about what was valued in the world in which I grew up. Tough boys, for sure, smart girls, not so much.

So it made sense to me when I read what Pulitzer Prize–winning poet Sharon Olds explained in a 2015 interview with Kaveh Akbar in his magazine *Divedapper*: that she, too, had grown up in an unartistic home and would go to church with her parents, hear the music and have for those few minutes each week access to beauty that she didn't find anywhere else in her suburban existence. How when she started listening to the radio she got excited by Top Forty hits, and then dancing at school dances became her art. This might not seem like much of a linchpin moment, but it was a quiet revelation to read her acknowledgement of these influences. I loved how unafraid Olds was to admit to these modest beginnings. I liked how she didn't waste any time avowing or disavowing religious beliefs or claiming grand influences, but said, plainly, that church music was what gave her that tiny, nearly impossible window on art. Most people won't admit to having so little that fifteen minutes a week meant so much, or having AM radio function as an early artistic muse. Most writers want to claim either more romantic forms of privation or more intellectual influences. I like how Olds didn't dress up the dullness of her suburban childhood culture, which was so much like mine.

We have not much to complain of, Olds and I, and maybe you as well; we were fed and clothed and stuck on the fringes of a consumer culture, far from art, and told it was enough. It is absolutely true that compared to childhoods of real economic and social privation in which people can't afford to eat that our beginnings are not dramatic or even startling. But that dull blend is exactly my point. Many people have had more daunting and sometimes awful upbringings: childhoods pierced by war or violence, shaped by racism and prejudice and poverty more abject than what my parents experienced. I am thinking especially about people who live under conditions of systemic racism and violence, and those whose poverty is not only not genteel but also state-sanctioned and generationally enforced. Oglala Lakota writer Layli Long Soldier's poem "Wahpánič̌a," from her book WHEREAS, is about the "punctuation of poverty," including "anyone asserting that poverty isn't about money has never been stomach-sick over how to spend their last

$3 ... on milk or gas or half for both with two children in the back-seat watching." So, with the spectrum of poverties and violences in the world, I offer the conditions of my upbringing not as evidence of special terribleness, but rather evidence of perhaps a familiar kind of upbringing, where thinking beyond your context was being snooty, or even worse, snotty. This was not so much a Tall Poppy Syndrome – in which the high-achieving are cut down to size by social criticism – than it was a No-Poppy Syndrome.

My parents tried to appear fit enough for city life; they succeeded, or succeeded enough, partly due to the class-striving that remained part of their awareness all their lives. If you subscribe to notions of cultural inheritance – and I am not always certain that I do – you might say that they were made for it. They came from a culture that has been historically invested in bloody-mindedness with the proven strategy of withstanding the inevitable deprivation by imperial overlords by depriving themselves first. The Scots are not the only culture with that tendency, and as immigrants to Canada they were more privileged than many other populations. And there's this historical problem: many Scots served as military or service personnel to the English, and thus were part of the militarized action against Indigenous people during the colonization of Upper Canada and the Northwest. How's that for a culturally chequered legacy, in which one's way out of deprivation is the militarized deprivation and abuse of others?

Both my maternal grandparents had been grindingly poor for generations. My mother's father joined the British army in 1914 because they promised him free boots and a warm coat and three meals a day. Such possessions, and guaranteed food, were beyond his wildest dreams. His enlistment photo shows a six-foot-four-inch painfully thin twenty-year-old, someone who was more than willing to be shot at if the army fed him. My grandmother was a maid-of-all-work in a respectable though not especially grand house in North Yorkshire, tiny as the actress who plays Daisy on *Downton Abbey*. They came to Canada in 1920. My father's parents came to Canada a little earlier, but my mother always said that she understood only about a third of what her father-in-law said. He was from the island of Mull off the west coast of Scotland, and had become a blacksmith because he loved horses. As a poor child on a rocky island, he knew that only the rich had horses, and when he discovered that he could be close to the creatures and earn a living, that was the ultimate job for him. The Great Depression was hard on both of my parents' large birth families in their tiny prairie towns where they did not, despite the advertisements that lured them to Canada, become farmers, because they had none of the skills. Their kids expected nothing, and received it in abundance.

But after the Depression and World War Two, during the economic recovery period, my parents worked and finagled their ways into white-collar jobs in which the hours were long and the work often menial, trying to make it in a small prairie city that was to them a vast metropolis. Most of the time, they met people much like themselves: people from very small towns who were crawling up the economic ladder and feeling genuinely grateful for the chance.

My parents must have run into people who scoffed at them, or were cruel about their hick backgrounds. I know I met such people once I was old enough to recognize them. I haven't forgotten the mother of a big-city friend and her reaction to hearing that I was from Winnipeg. She launched into a five-minute monologue about what a "terrible city" it was, how bad the restaurants were, and how all the people were just ignorant farmers and "there were so many Natives." It froze me to the spot. She went on as I stood in my wet socks in her cold kitchen, a guest in her home. This speech was meant to shame me, to remind me that she was aware of my humble origins. She may not have known how right she was, that members of my father's family farmed and I had relatives by marriage who had Indigenous heritages. I was not yet savvy enough to think of shaming her for her racism and classism, but knew that I was either supposed to agree with her or defend myself, and that she was unnerved when I did neither. I didn't claim another heritage or background; I didn't suggest that I was a cut above her expectations. I let her freak out about my unsuitability. I knew I frightened her. She thought that I was an ambitious class contagion on two long legs, and her invocation of her high standards and sophisticated tastes was her way of protecting herself from me, her way of telling me that there was not a snowball's chance in hell of me getting hold of her nice house, which I knew already.

*

I was over thirty before I understood – despite my excellent undergraduate GPA – that I could study for a graduate degree. My parents were not so sure. They were supportive but suspicious, a state confirmed so often that I should have had T-shirts made up for them to wear: *Supportive but suspicious. Because you should be careful.* My parents were often guarded on my behalf, thinking that disappointment was in the offing, accompanied by the inevitable discovery that I would not get a gentle introduction to a difficult-to-navigate system, and that I would be hurt by the experience. They were worried that I wasn't smart in the ways that those other kids – doctors' and lawyers' kids with money – were smart. My parents weren't interested in smashing the system; they were too aware of how they had been allowed in the back door. They also didn't want to see me crushed by challenging it.

But because I would and did enter into a system where my parents could not protect me, they devised their own strategies to account for me. They invented a shared myth that I'd had a "rough start" to my studies, which was going to take a lot of hard work and determination to overcome. I have no idea from where this myth originated. It could have been something I said in a phone call home, a crack I had made about "working my brain to the bone" or just as easily fabricated from something they heard about someone else. The fiction of my "rough start" and subsequent need for a lot of hard work to catch up to those *really* smart people fit my parents' idea of how things got done: by dogged persistence rather than brilliance, and hard-won self-discipline above all. My parents were accountably brave. Their bravery is transmuted into me as my imagination.

*

My father's father operated a forge in which he heated, bent, pounded and otherwise moulded metal into horseshoes, farm equipment and other implements. Family legend has it that he became a farrier in the army when it was assumed by a higher-up that since he was a rural boy he knew about horses. He didn't, but, charged with taking care of them, discovered that the longer he worked with the horses, the more he liked them. From then on he worked to be with the horses as much as he could, and became a blacksmith in civilian life. I don't know whether this is 100 per cent true, but it's the story my father always told, and many years ago it meshed in my mind with a sequence from Timothy Findley's novel *The Wars*, so much so that I could see my grandfather in the ship's hold with the horses on the way to the battlefields in France, even though my father never told the story that way. My father has moulded the fragments of my grandfather's life into a story and I have added to it, looking for cohesion, making story from what materials I had available. Blacksmiths know that heat bends iron to the right shapes for tools; writers know that it's necessary to bend materials into shapes. The longer I work as an artist, the more the mind at work seems like a heated forge. I know that the popular metaphor for the brain at work is a computer, but in artmaking we heat the material: tell the truth but tell it slant, as Emily Dickinson said. As we forge individual pieces, so too we forge a method and gradually mould an artistic practice.

The idea of forging an artistic practice while reading only the map made from our own desire lines is a pretty powerful one. Scraping an artistic practice together error by discovery by error is hard work, especially when you are told that art is not for the likes of you. So I believed that I needed to change in order to make art, or at least I believed it enough to leave home, move to a big city and get a university education so that if I couldn't make art I could at least sidle up to it and take a good look. I wanted to be smart and I wanted to be sophisticated. I also wanted to be independent, and that was maybe the best impulse – and, unexpectedly, my most artistic one.

Independence is a good thing for young artists to strive toward for the excellent reason that being an artist, especially when you are working class or any kind of outsider, means that you have to push against a lot of ideas about what's valuable and what is not. My parents worried about how I would make my way through the world, something that makes more sense to me now that I am older. When I was young, though, it felt like a millstone around my neck and a deep plot to thwart my selfhood. That brings me to another good thing to have as a beginner artist: a dose of arrogance, a beneficial degree of self-confidence in your ability to go places and do things. Sometimes even blissful ignorance can be a good substitute for confidence; many people who are too naive to know that things are not done a certain way get those same things done by showing up and asking.

But writers also need readers; actors need audiences; singers need musicians and venues; and everyone needs to know someone else who does what you do and does it better. This could be a mentor, but peers can also be great teachers – maybe even the best teachers. My style and subject matters were formed through years of workshops and reading and peer discussion and having generous writer friends and submitting lots of work to literary journals. I also studied for my master's and doctoral degrees in my thirties, and remember well the force of being constantly graded, judged, assessed and professionalized. Those experiences are similar in some ways to taking an MFA degree, but aren't quite the same as working intensely on a creative manuscript in a cohort watched over by senior writers.

I wrote alone for a long time, and only occasionally showed people my work because the reactions I received were generally so embarrassing. This may have been because the writing wasn't very good, but I got the sense then, and believe it now, that people were also embarrassed that I was writing anything at all, as though my audacity was a spectacle, a public shouting. Moving to the Big City didn't make me an artist. I still needed to find my people, and I had no idea where – or who – they would be. I was still a striving-class girl without connections or mentors. I needed to hear from someone who knew a thing or two. I needed a writing community, but didn't know it. Then one day my friend Tamara said, "Maybe you'd like my friend's book. It's excellent." Tamara had already recommended terrific non-fiction to me, and so I picked up the poetry book she recommended and heard the sound of a window sliding open. The book was Anne Michaels' *The Weight of Oranges* and the image from the title poem, a wet paper grocery bag splitting from the weight of oranges in a Toronto kitchen in winter, was so strongly evocative of my present that I snapped awake.

I knew, in my new wakefulness, that I couldn't do it alone anymore; I registered for Susan Ioannou's poetry class at the Toronto Board's Continuing Education, and later for Helen Humphreys' workshop at George Brown, both places where my spinning wheels found traction. Other poets kindly brought me in from the open field of my own raging assumptions and spoke to me like I might know what I was doing. I did not, but to this day I bless them for acting as though I did. They became peers with real expectations to whom I was responsible. I remain grateful to Susan for her unflappable welcome and her file folder crammed with writing exercises, and to Helen who a few years later said to me, without warning, "You have a manuscript sitting in a drawer, right? You should be sending it out." I was too stunned to tell Helen the truth – that my scattered poems were not anything close to a "manuscript" – so I just nodded. Then I went home and started thinking of the poems as a manuscript, because if Helen thought I had a manuscript in my desk drawer, then by God I would make it true. That was me trying to figure out how to be a writer and taking my cues from anyone who dropped one. The manuscript – after much revision, rearranging and shuffling of poems, and after a few years of hearing publishers say not "no," but that they would not even read it so don't send it to them – became my first book, *holding ground*. Though it would be nicely dramatic to say that I produced a book because I had promised Helen, I don't know what would have happened to those poems had I not said out loud to a writer I revered that I had a manuscript.

People generally don't realize that many accomplished writers don't have regular day jobs and often teach in all kinds of places and under all kinds of circumstances: continuing education, colleges, arts organizations, prisons, writer's circles in bookstores. Every slam performance is a workshop in gesture, every reading a crash course in community building. Beginners should worry less about what organization is offering which course than they do the writing credentials of the instructor. Of course, I didn't do that when I took my first poetry workshop. I was not that savvy. I was not even careful. Because I knew that I would talk myself out of it if I slowed down for one second, I registered on impulse, did not research the instructor and showed up to the first class with a chip on my shoulder, acting as though I knew everything. If someone had asked me how exactly I was "better than" anyone else, I would have been hard-pressed to come up with any evidence. I fooled exactly no one. Threatened with new experiences, I relied on my strong past record of knowing how to get out while the getting was good. I arrived at the class ready to chuck it all if anything made me too uncomfortable.

Thinking about it now, I can't say what could have made me less comfortable than I had already made myself. In the face of my attitude, the warm and welcoming Susan Ioannou offered her deep love for poetry and didn't bat an eyelash. She urged us all to read Canadian poetry and to write, no matter what. The chip on my shoulder didn't last long, composed as it was of my shyness and general class-passing anxiety. I came back for the next week and the next, bringing poems each time, my Type-A personality kicking into overdrive when Susan gave us writing exercises. A task! I love tasks! At last, I was distracted from the paralyzing force of my own discomfort by the chance to write to a deadline.

That first workshop was a revelation. What I remember most about it was the way it made me feel. I floated over the Bloor Viaduct at the end of the evening, my head full of poems and talk and what I was thinking of writing for the next week. This was in the years before the Luminous Veil was installed on the bridge, and my walk included a wide and unobstructed view of the Don River Valley. The viaduct seemed literary in itself, a landmark because of its place in the opening pages of the most Torontonian novel I knew: Michael Ondaatje's *In the Skin of A Lion*. The open space, the green valley with the sinuous river, the sensation of being suspended above it all and the rush of words in my head: all that became a symbol of what I wanted to move forward into. Susan had reminded me of the strange language of my inner life.

Such a poetic heaven didn't stick around forever. The more I worked on becoming a better writer, the more writers I met. It wasn't always a love fest. I met writers from all kinds of backgrounds, and some were great peer mentors to me; they had experiences and educations beyond mine, and kindly shepherded my poems along in workshops, praising some parts and gently recommending revisions to others while offering tips and books to read. Sometimes egos crashed around the room, and it was awful. Sometimes people were competitive, and sometimes those very same people turned around and were incredibly generous. There were arguments, sometimes driven by aesthetics and politics, sometimes by fear and run-of-the-mill nastiness, and sometimes about privilege. A lot of the time I simply listened. Some of the time I spoke and acquitted myself well, and other times I was in way over my head and stammering.

This kind of grassroots artistic moulding is a far cry from the MFA experience, but I liked my Choose Your Own Adventure education in writing. It happened at the right time for me and I didn't go into debt because of it. I made connections and met people and started doing readings, sitting on boards of organizations and getting to know how things worked. I sent poems out for publication: some got picked up, others didn't. By the time Helen asked me about the manuscript in my drawer, I was ready to think about my poems that way. I couldn't have drawn a map to getting a poetry manuscript published back then, and I can barely discern the pattern in hindsight.

*

Say for the sake of argument that you are at the very beginning of your artistic inquiry. You know that what you want is different than what you've found so far, but you have not had much of a chance to figure out what "different" could mean.

You may live in small-town Canada. You may live on First Nations traditional lands, like Six Nations in southwestern Ontario or Kahnawake on the shores of the St. Lawrence River, or in another kind a cultural community that maintains conscious separation from the great blur of Canadian urban culture: Mennonite in southern Manitoba, Sikh in BC's Lower Mainland or hundreds of other communities and cultures all over Canada. You might live in the suburbs of a bigger city: Woodbridge or White Rock or Lachine. You are thinking about writing or acting or singing, and about the future, and you might feel a little panicked, rudderless or resigned. You might be political and working to make a difference. When you ask a question about how you might make a life in art, it's not casual or cynical or ingenuous, and it's okay not to know.

Art is so good; I know why it's kept a mystery.

Desert Island of
Genius

The image of the writer sequestered in their garret is an enduring image even now when, with a tablet and a wifi connection, anywhere can be your garret. This image feeds the fantasy of independence, self-reliance and isolated genius that remains attached to the idea of the creative process. But the term *isolated genius* is an oxymoron. Even when we work without anyone else in the room, we still work in tandem with our peers, the cultural conceptions of what good poetry or good painting or good singing is; with teachers and texts and writers we've never met; with spiritual or intellectual mentors; or maybe with people whose restrictive cultural norms we are trying to defy. Contribution is key, as is having the courage to row away from the desert island of "genius."

Writers are often shy or introverted people. The myth of the isolated genius feels attractive because it makes our (sometimes desired) isolation appear as though it is solely a function of one's superior brain rather than related to loneliness or social awkwardness. Who wants to admit to those? It's so socially awkward to admit to social awkwardness. As Yvonne Blomer, Poet Laureate of Victoria, puts it when discussing her years as a beginner writer, she wanted most to learn not how to choose the right word but something more practical: "How to speak to my instructors and not feel like a dolt. I was very scared in that first class so it seemed it must be important. Poetry knocked my socks off and I just wanted to be able to create a feeling the way I was made to feel by other poets. Could I do that?" The benefit of remaining isolated as an artist is that you never have to feel the kind of anxiety Yvonne describes, and you would never have to pay attention to anyone else's art; you could even get away with refusing to acknowledge that anyone else even makes art. But this will not work for long. As writer and professor Kit Dobson notes, "Art is a fantastic conversation, and it is absolutely a life-and-death conversation. Becoming part of it is in fact shockingly simple: all that it seems to me to call for is a willingness to witness the art around us, to interact with it and to respond to it in some way. Art does not happen in a vacuum, and don't assume that one can be a great artist without first becoming part of the conversation – join in and then discover what you can contribute."

When I was young, the party line was that if you wanted to make art (be an actor, writer or painter), then you had to leave the smaller place to be "taken seriously," and I was determined to be taken seriously at all costs. The irony of this is profound, considering that the small city I was from fostered a thriving arts community including a strong film group, an internationally acclaimed ballet school, two literary magazines, many local galleries and at least five professors of creative writing who were widely published and great instructors, including internationally known novelist, poet and father of Canadian postmodernism Robert Kroetsch. But this was also a time when the grouchy snobbery of excuse-makers occupied a lot of public discourse, and when you are a newbie looking for direction, you might get some bad advice. I didn't even know that such local resources existed, so I nearly shouted, "Hello, bad advice! Nice to meet you! Will you be my constant companion for years?" There is no formula for figuring out who to listen to and who to trust, which is another reason why maintaining a broad and deep artistic community is so important.

There are accepted practical reasons for moving far from one's home place, some of which are entwined with capitalism and colonialism. We sometimes move to where the work is, despite the fact that it takes us away from our families and cultural heritage and home environments. Or we listen to the culturally approved stories about upward mobility and about a united country, and it's easy to believe that that kind of identity – young, upwardly mobile Canadian – will stand in for family. This can replace other thoughts we might have, about loyalty or duty or service to the community, and insidiously so. Maybe it doesn't have to. My Indigenous students often refer to needing to go home for ceremonies, for community celebrations or for service work. So do students from other backgrounds. I admire their sense of belonging and ongoing participation in community in part because my own roots were so easily yanked up.

Many of us come to art fragile or apprehensive or incredulous, but somehow emboldened to try it despite its oddness, despite the fact that we have very little context for how it is supposed to work or how we are supposed to do it. The fresh start that artmaking can represent is real: a true mental refuge. It's no real surprise that many of us equate that with a geographical shift. While leaving one place and going to another might mean dragging all your problems with you, it can also mean – especially when you are young – a very potent new beginning. Most of us place a certain amount of faith in what artmaking will do for us, sometimes as a ticket to move us away from where we are, sometimes as a way to stay in one place but make our worlds larger. We may have ties to our community from which we want respite, though we may not be interested in completely cutting ourselves off from the home place.

One of the problems of relocating, whether to a big city or another small place that is not your home place, is the iron tang of isolation that you will taste living life far from your context. This may or may not turn into a useful solitary practice. The ability to drop a personal cone of silence onto your practice and do the work without reward or feedback is a valuable skill. It is also a skill that is nearly unexplainable to others; many will chafe against your ability to turn away from the world and toward your practice because they have no context for understanding it. Others may refuse to acknowledge its value. And in our super-connected twenty-first century, "alone" is relative: many of us make art in places full of people and noise. Solitary is a state of mind.

This idea of a solitary practice may seem to contradict the need for community, but they are two streams that feed into one another. Solitary practice is not the same as isolation for fear or from snobbery, and it is not the same as an investment in isolated genius. The myth of the isolated genius has been made popular via the media's promotion of a handful of writers who claim to be beyond the need for peers, and by decades of literary criticism invested in the assertion that genius requires no explanation and no context. The truth is more realistic and less romantic. Even Thoreau had neighbours at Walden Pond.

Whose Line Is It Anyway? Practice Makes Practice

one of the first things that i remember about myself is a thirst
to understand why so many people are so very unhappy and
so unkind to themselves and others. and i think i only realized
how unhappy the people around me during my childhood were
after reading novels … i remember having a lot trouble believing that actual people wrote novels: they were so magical! they
contained worlds! they *were* worlds!

    – a. charlie peters

What causes dazzle? A willingness to be dazzled.

    – Pearl Pirie

In 1976, Margaret Gibson wrote a short story called "Making It" in
her book *The Butterfly Ward*. The plot concerned a young, preg-
nant, schizophrenic woman and a gay man living together in a

crappy apartment in Toronto and taking care of each other as each figures out what it takes to "make it." That title was expunged when it was made into a 1977 film called *Outrageous!* starring Craig Russell and Hollis McLaren, and I have always been sorry about that because I thought the title was the most curious part of the story. What was "making it" in Toronto in the 1970s? What was being made? The French language has it right, I think, in *faire*: a single verb for "to do or to make." To do is to make and to make is to do. Lots of us figure out on our own that we like being able to access our creativity as much as possible, but it's much harder to live like it's yours and keep going for more than a few months in the face of every other obligation you have.

And there's something else, something insidious in corporate culture that wants to use creativity and insult it, too. Cheery admonitions of "no budget to do the impossible, you are just going to have to *get creative!*" skewer the creative force as a last-ditch solution. Creativity is a real skill. As an artist, you need to develop the capacity to turn your creativity off and on, not so much like a spigot but like how we juggle places to be and responsibilities to be completed. You learn to write to meet deadlines so that you can pay bills and complete long projects; you learn how to stop writing at four o'clock so you can pick up your kids or run errands; you may even learn to write only for twenty minutes at a time when your life allows only those short spurts. Too many offhand commands to "work your magic by four o'clock" can deaden anyone's practice. That said, we do our artistic practices a disservice when we treat them as delicate hothouse plants. Creativity is a muscle; it can seem flabby if you are not used to using it, if you are still working out how and when to flex it.

*

When I teach a writing course, I spend a lot of time writing individual comments for the beginner writers – a lot of time. New artists need to know that they are *doing it*; that is, that they are creating something that is readable in the way they've planned, or that gets an unanticipated response that sparks discussion. New writers need to know that not only are they doing it, but also that they will be trusted to do it again soon. Reactions to feedback are varied: some people are surprised to receive it even though I've told them to expect my tiny ink marks all over their page.

But what happens next is a curious mix of shock and delight. This is often people's first experience of being read, of being treated as a writer with things to say and methods with which to say them and a responsibility to a readership – even a readership of one. A very specific kind of silence descends on the room as people read what I've written about their work; it's a silence like no other. Inside it, standing at its epicentre, I can hear the years of ridicule falling away, the years of receiving only checkmarks and "good effort!" as comments on diction or structure or imagery over which the writer has agonized. The absorbed silence of a roomful of people reading feedback on their work practically rings with the internal chime of *ohmigod ohmigod*. New writers are starved for attention to their work. Even at the very beginning of the beginning, they know without being told that this is hard to come by.

I usually distribute drafts with my written feedback at the end of each class, mindful that some people wish to get their drafts and leave the room to read over the notes in private, but lately I have noticed a different trend. More writers have been staying put, to read what I've written in the classroom, minutes ticking by as I quietly erase the board, pack my briefcase and put on my coat. The silence continues until I have to gently remind them that the class has ended, that others are waiting outside to use our classroom, that our turn and this week's class are both over. Still, some writers will stretch out the feedback experience, reading and rereading, or asking me what a word means. Some of that is about not being able to read my handwriting, and some, I suspect, is because people want to hear me say what I've written: "evocative" or "intriguing" or "you don't need this line"; "logic" and "word choice?" and "contradictory." Once, years ago now, I walked down three flights of stairs to the echoing soundtrack of a student reading my written paragraph of feedback aloud to a friend, both of them perched on the stairwell of the floor above. My sentences floated down on me as I descended, an odd benediction and an aural reminder of my responsibility to write well when I write feedback. It was, strangely, like hearing the inside of my own head broadcast on a private radio channel. But while I had written the words, they had become that writer's right to trumpet or to bury, as she wished.

At the outset of your writing practice, before you have been in a classroom or workshop atmosphere, you may be surprised by the force of having your work read by peers. The happy shock of this should never be underestimated. The first few times someone pays attention to your writing, the experience is like a drug – or like having a two-tonne weight dropped on you. Workshopping a piece of writing is simultaneously an outrageous compliment and your worst nightmare. I watch it happen, and the faces around the room change: from suspicious scowls, to careful apprehension and keeping one's face blank, to openness, smiling, even belly laughs. Many beginner writers will disavow their wish for an audience and impulsively want to keep their writing private, but many end up loving the audience that they find in those first serious readers. And so confidence grows, from resistance to reluctance to disbelief to glee to possibility to working community.

After a few weeks, the new writers get a bit addicted to being read, and when there's a week where I have scheduled a different exercise,

there are complaints. "A week without feedback? Why write anything?" one beginner writer kvetched, only half kidding. At the end
of the course, I field instructions from students to incorporate more
feedback into the proceedings, because what they have received
doesn't feel like enough. It never will be enough because our egos
are insatiable, but this is a fair enough reaction from writers who
have just discovered the rewards of an intelligent audience. Every
rags-to-riches story, of becoming famous and adored for your bestseller, relies on the fantasy of money and a sea of undifferentiated
faces as your audience. It is, at its root, a fantasy of getting love
without having to give it: not unusual in a celebrity-obsessed society,
but not really in concert with an artistic practice. So when I note
that another reward of a community is the attention of an intelligent audience, I mean an audience that rewards effort and gives
feedback. It is reciprocal, and it wears the many faces of one's peers.
Most beginner writers don't know that this is possible and, without
knowing it, it turns out to be what they crave.

The responsibility—and the pleasure—of reading the work of
others should be modelled first by a senior artist, and then passed
bit by bit to beginner writing peers. In my classes, I ask the students to take what I have done and imitate that attention in a group
peer-assessment exercise. This takes the greedy energy of craving
discussion about the work and siphons it into small-group feedback. For some beginner writers, it is their first taste of literary
community. Students give each other feedback, emulating my style
at first and then branching out as they get to know each other's
work and gain more confidence in their abilities.

When first practicing any art, you move ahead on instinct. If
you have had bad experiences trusting your instincts, this might be
painful or scary. If you have had experiences trusting your instincts
that turned out well, you move forward with a little more confidence and speed. If you have been told that only people who don't

look and sound like you get to make art, you may barely move at all. Or you may charge forward on the energy of defiance. But whatever the case, gaining ground is going to be relative.

Doing something new is a head-filling experience, and it is often hard to discern, in all the internal static, whether or not you have accomplished what you set out to do. If the task is to run across a field of flames without catching on fire yourself, you will know if you have done it when you are standing on the opposite side of the field, scorched but otherwise unharmed. When you compare very measurable, very perceivable goals, like not catching on fire, to something more ephemeral, like writing a poem using an extended metaphor or harmonizing a cappella or getting the timing right in a comedy bit, it's harder to tell if you are indeed doing it, so it's good to have someone to ask. There is only so much inching along in the dark that most people are willing to do in order to move forward. It helps if you can see evidence, from your group leader and from your peers: scratch marks on the page, the conductor's smile when you get the timing right on your entrance, the rest of the cast crowding the rehearsal hall when you work on the big scene. These moments say, "You're doing it. I see it here and here and here and especially here. Keep going, see how far you can get by next week."

Running with the Elbower: A True Fable

When I was learning to run, I trained alone. I was writing a dissertation and a poetry book and I kept odd hours. This suited me, but it meant that I ran for an hour usually after writing all day. I was also not a good runner, and a bit embarrassed at my style and lack of speed. At that time, I really wanted privacy to build up the length of time and distance I could run. But six months into doing it alone, I felt ready for a little public running event. I was ready to withstand a bit of criticism, to be instructed on how to do it better, to be among my peers and my superiors who were doing what I was trying to do and doing it much better than I was. I didn't think that running a five-kilometre route with others in a charity fundraiser would be competitive; my only goal was to finish in approximately the practice time I had been maintaining, and to make good on the promise I had made to my pledges to finish the run.

What I didn't foresee is how I'd be dropped right into an instant community. From the moment we started to the finish line, I could feel the other runners around me, many faster and some slower, but, almost without exception, they were all encouraging. Some yelled as we ran together, *go go go!*; some applauded and cheered everyone around them, and me, too, as it didn't seem to matter whether we knew each other or not. I have never seen so many big goofy grins in a crowd. I said almost without exception because there was one guy who bolted forward, actively elbowing other runners out of his way. If you've ever run with a thousand other people, you know that there's an etiquette to things that even beginners like me could perceive in a matter of seconds. Serious competitors take the front few rows and everyone else, no matter where they start in the crowd, knows that it will really only be a matter of a dozen strides until they find themselves among runners of approximately the same fitness and experience. With these people, you can run companionably, moving at your own pace, private and public at once. There is never any need to jostle anyone.

But the Elbower busted on through, incredulous and insulted at the proximity of so many everyday runners. We all noticed, especially since he shot ahead at a breakneck pace I thought was ambitious for a five-kilometre run. Even the front-runners, who I saw at the start, didn't try to move at that kind of pace. But I was a beginner: What did I know? A woman running beside me had no such qualms; she was in her sixties, all lean muscle and experience, and she muttered, "What an asshole," at the Elbower's back. She was a much better runner than I was and soon outpaced me with her long stride. I could only watch admiringly. I then fell in with a woman with dark hair that reached the centre of her back and a henna tattoo on the back of her right hand. We paced each other and people passed us; we passed others. Then the one-kilometre marker came up and everyone whooped and there were tables with water and volunteers cheering and we waved and ran past – and that's when I saw him, flat out on his back on the grass, chest heaving dramatically, like a cartoon of a runner: the Elbower. I only caught a glimpse before we blew by in a grinning, panting herd and I never saw him again. I was told once that as a runner it didn't matter if you had speed or even style, but that you needed to train in order to have stamina. And, I thought as I headed for the two-kilometre marker with the hennaed runner beside me, you need to know how to resist acting like an asshole.

Running depends on the smart use of adrenaline and setting reachable goals, among other things, and so does making art. I don't mean the high-octane adrenaline of surviving a brush with death, but it's not uncommon to feel a bit dizzy after writing. Years ago I drove to the airport to pick up a writer friend, and she came down the escalator with a big grin on her face and said, "I am a writing machine!" because she had spent the flight without a seat-mate, without interruption, without a child to look after, writing for four hours. When I attended Natalie Goldberg's workshop in the 1990s, each time someone volunteered to read aloud their work from the freewriting session, Natalie said when they were done, "You might feel a little high from that later." My friend and I looked at each other the third time she said this and I cracked wise ("Is that a requirement? What if I don't feel high?") until I realized that she didn't want anyone to have the experience without warning. She took her responsibility as a senior writer seriously, and cared less about sounding repetitive than making sure she cared for the people who took the risk reading to 150 strangers. She was saying, "You are doing it. You just did it. I saw you. I heard you."

I Confess, and Other Social Negotiations

Artists will talk about drive. We talk about what will sustain you through the long hours alone, in front of your easel or screen. We talk about being compelled, about having fire in the belly, about telling a story that needs to be told and dozens of other "must-dos" for writers and other artists. But remember that most of the time, when you hear artists talk about these "must-dos" and "must-haves," they are being interviewed or they are teaching. Those "must-dos" are, at least partially, rhetorical constrictions: phrases and words and assertions designed to offer a method that will place a comprehensible frame on what seems, to non-artists, incomprehensible. I don't mean to say that these pieces of advice are bad or false; I subscribe to many of them myself. But for every writer who claims an all-consuming passion for narrative or a fiery, lyrical imagination, there is another who knows only that they want to write in order to reshape their reality, to imagine other worlds, to be elsewhere via writing or a hundred other unexpressed and inexpressible reasons. There's not a thing wrong with having humble reasons for writing. It's true that a writer's life, as with many arts, is lonely, and having a strong motivation to keep writing is a good thing. But hearing tropes of determination trumpeted as though writing is always and only about going into battle mode can be wearying. Even a description of the inside of one's head will sound to others like chaos, or a lie.

It's hard to say if confession is a myth or a motivator when it comes to making art. It is not the job of the senior artist to dictate subject matter for the beginner writer, but only to offer ways, means and possibilities. In *The History of Sexuality*, Michel Foucault notes that we're compelled to confess – the idea of "sins" being implicit in his phrasing – and that is not by accident. Foucault was describing a psychology and a cultural history shaped by a Catholic belief system, and within that system the compulsion to confess makes sense. But the confessional mode in artmaking exists as both promise and problem. Some beginner writers are eager to write their world into shape and substance via confession, and others are equally determined to resist laying claim to any such feelings. It is fashionable lately in certain artistic circles to disdain confessional work, and in others to exalt it as "more authentic, more real" than other work. While I understand both these positions, when it comes to beginner artists, I have concerns about disavowing previously unspoken experience, especially when writing such work allows those whose perspectives have been sidelined, silenced or marginalized to write their reality. People who don't believe that naming has power are very privileged indeed. This is not to say that confession is a requirement, for there are salacious implications there, too. Emotions can be and are the subject of a lot of poetry, but emotion needn't be the subject matter. Consider the way Dionne Brand works with news reports in *Inventory*, or how Claudia Rankine analyzes sports reporting and race in *Citizen*. There are trial transcripts in Soraya Peerbaye's *Tell*, nineteenth-century history in Wayde Compton's *49th Parallel Psalm* and cloud formation in Lisa Robertson's *The Weather*. None of these books are the least bit emotionless, but each of them complicates the idea that art is solely about an individual's private and affective experience of the self, published or displayed for the delectation of others.

That said, there's no denying the draw of a confessional impulse for many beginner artists. I note that people are not drawn to its sensational subject matter so much as to how that subject matter lives on the page: studded with a range of affect, the rawness of experience honed and placed with care in the completed work. I understand that it feels incredible to see what "could not be said," published in black ink on a white page before one's very eyes. For example, reading Sylvia Plath's words, "Daddy, daddy, you bastard,

I'm through," is not a salacious thrill but a political one in the best sense: evidence that someone somewhere has wrestled the law into their own form and thrown it back into the face of the tyrant. The face of the tyrant is, as Plath points out, often a family member, and sometimes even someone who is loved as terribly as they are hated – for what else could fuel that fury but that mix for which there is no English word, that nauseating swirl of need and fury that can stifle us. Hearing it declared – in art, public, polished, bold – is a revelation for many. I know it was for me.

One of the difficult parts of learning something new is the inability to see the big picture, the pattern in the mosaic, the machine rather than the million moving parts. One of the hardest parts – especially if you like being in control – is not knowing what you are doing but doing it anyway. Apparent contradiction is good for art. Moments of deep contradiction, affective or linguistic or logical, are honoured in art, certainly in lyric forms but also in more experimental styles. I think of bpNichol's lifelong work with *H*, the first letter in the alphabet of his personal mythos, a position that may have grown from biographical circumstances, which in Nichol's case was growing up in Winnipeg's Wildwood Park suburb, where the streets were so new that they were given letters before being named; Nichol lived on H Street. His career-long play with *H* as the ur-letter, the shaping force of language, led him to serious consideration of the arbitrariness of language forms. Nichol is a great example of an artist who followed an impulse that appeared whimsical or nonsensical, and forged an aesthetic from his serious play that both supported and negated the concept of the originary moment.

You get to choose your subject matter, and you also get to refuse to listen to people who say that it's too slight/too specific/too esoteric/too banal. For years I couldn't have declared what my poetic subject was; I had a space more than a subject, and a style more than a narrative. I just wanted to go into that space as often as possible.

I couldn't have said why or declared a style or subject for myself. This is 100 per cent okay when you are starting out. In fact, it's 100 per cent okay even if you are many years into your artistic practice.

Making It, Doing It

When I was a young performer, I worked with a director who always used the phrase *doin' it* to praise the actor who was giving him the performance he wanted. The phrase sounded perpetually capitalized and italicized: *Doin' It*. The director usually issued the phrase in rehearsal like this: "Joe is up there *Doin' It*. I don't know what the rest of you are doin'. But you're not *Doin' It*." The director's tastes were pronounced, and as time went by, we became used to being told over and over that some people were unequivocally "*Doin' It*," while the rest of us, including many people who went on to have very successful careers, were categorically NOT "*Doin' It*." In the face of these daily reminders, our impulse to mount a counter-competition was surprisingly healthy. Which of us could elicit the most vehement negation from the director? Who could imitate his expostulations the best, and who could be told with the most frequency to get off the stage? It was perhaps fitting that the most legendary of all imitations was performed not by any one of us, but rendered as "yooou think yerr dyooooin' it, but yerr not dyooooin' it," out of the mouth of our quiet stage manager, who repeated the howler of a phrase in a part-Swedish part-Scots accent with which neither she nor the director spoke. We begged her to say it again and again, which she did, with a tiny satisfied smile.

Negative examples can be valuable, if only to make us feel lucky to have the communities we do. Beginner artists need to know that they can survive all kinds of crap, including bad instruction. I was told publicly, frequently and in no uncertain terms early in my artistic career that I was not doin' it, and I lived to tell the tale and still make art. I offer this story not as advice to instructors – though let me take a moment to say that public shaming is not and never will be good pedagogy – but rather as evidence that cohorts can support each other through the most ridiculous negativity and find solidarity, humour and even, perversely, hope. That hope comes from community, from learning not to believe everything you hear and from practice.

A poet friend of mine who also teaches high school had a very talented student who was writing incendiary, sophisticated poems, and he recommended her for writing workshops and national student prizes. She eventually won a prestigious contest. She came to him in June of her final year in high school and said, referring to her big win, "*Now* do I get to be a writer?" My friend, who knew all about the instabilities of publishing, didn't know what to say about her future. He wasn't going to warn her as she was graduating from high school about every way that writing could disappoint her. He didn't want to be that naysayer. He said instead, "You are already a writer." Many writers have a moment like that seared into their memory: the first time they heard someone say this – a published writer, an instructor, a mentor – and it's often long before their first publication in a magazine or a book. The statement can mark the start of an artistic life.

The Doubtful

When you are writing, glance over your shoulder, and you'll
find there is no reader. Just you and the page. Feel lonely? Good.
　– Richard Hugo, *The Triggering Town*

For me, the impulse to work things out on the page is perpetual,
even when I don't give in to this impulse. When you first start
writing, you will probably feel alone, and this itself can feel heady:
possibly permissive, maybe scary, likely freeing. Hugo's warning,
above, is also a directive, and not a cruel one: he's preparing us for
the future. He is recognizing the solitary impulse with a solitary
confirmation. Many of us live in our heads, maintaining what is
sometimes called a "rich inner life," almost always mockingly. But
a rich inner life sustains many people, and those who mock it can
only be jealous of the resilience that this inner life affords the thinker.
It saves people again and again. You have to go somewhere when
you have nowhere to go.

　Anne Sexton, when she was just starting to write, brought to a
university professor something she had written while listening to
the stereo in her living room. She asked him, "What is this? Is this
a poem?" When I first read about this incident, and read the piece,

long after Sexton's death and long after she had won the Pulitzer Prize in 1967 for *Live or Die*, I read her hesitancy as ingenuous, but that was ungenerous of me. Not everyone can tell, or at least not right away, what art is. The piece was indeed a poem, and became a famous one in the Sexton oeuvre: "Music Swims Back to Me." But if our expectations are that poems rhyme, then perhaps "Music Swims Back to Me" is not a poem. If you have been taught that poetry is never written by women but only by long-dead British men, then you wouldn't recognize many contemporary poets. I liked that Sexton, like Sharon Olds, was unafraid to reveal her naive ideas: to say *I don't know* and be willing to claim that unsure moment.

It's easy to pretend you always knew what you now know. It's easy, but it isn't always accurate and it isn't always kind. Good teaching or good mentoring involves letting people know that the work of artmaking is lifelong, and includes encountering doubt. Doubt is often disconcerting, but it does not need to be devastating. That is another good thing to let beginners know: that doubt does not mean despair, or giving up, but a need to shake things up. Change your position at the table, in the room and in the world, the place you take in the order or in the chaos of your own or someone else's making.

For example, today: the term is starting and I have a very full head. I am writing in the only twenty minutes I have free in a day crammed with responsibilities. I am writing longhand in my notebook, in the quad at a picnic table, the day before fall classes begin. The space itself couldn't be more public, and the students who think me not writerly enough ought to get a load of this act of public writing, but none of them happen by. It's one of those Ontario September days with a wind so dry and hot it'll suck the air right out of your lungs. I keep writing these sentences, but the logjam is not moving. My full head remains full. The more I write, the more it becomes clear that I can't spill it onto the page.

The start of term has all the anticipation and anxieties of a new start. And I have yet another piece of history feeding into this professional anxiety: tomorrow is the anniversary of my mother's death. All week I have felt, as I feel each year at this time, the hourly chimes of the long days of her dying, those weeks I spent in the hospital and in her empty house in heat exactly like this. The prairie quality of this dry wind feels fateful, a stiff calendrical hand on my shoulder. For the rest of my teaching life, the beginning of the term and the end of my mother's life will coincide in the same September week, layered like sedimentary rock and as studded with tiny fossil forms. Worse things and better things will happen, maybe very soon: all unforeseen today.

I look over my shoulder, and know Richard Hugo is right: there's no reader there waiting for me to solve this moment. I feel doubtful. It's good.

The Writer Next Door:
A Finding Place

When people say that poetry is a luxury, or an option, or for the educated middle classes, or that it shouldn't be read at school because it is irrelevant, or any of the strange and stupid things that are said about poetry and its place in our lives, I suspect that the people doing the saying have had things pretty easy. A tough life needs a tough language – and that is what poetry is. That is what literature offers – a language powerful enough to say how it is.

It isn't a hiding place. It is a finding place.
– Jeanette Winterson, *Why Be Happy When You Could Be Normal?*

When I first read this, I felt as though Winterson had reached out, placed her finger on that hollow place at the top of my clavicle and pushed firmly. I felt seen, unequivocally, and with that, powerful enough to say how it was. But I had felt this before: I remember reading Audre Lorde's "Poetry is Not a Luxury," the essay to which

Winterson alludes, and Adrienne Rich's "When We Dead Awaken: Writing as Revision," and feeling the same fleeting alignment of brain and body, the same finding place. The very first time this happened, I was a lot younger.

That July, I was fourteen and visiting my lifelong bestie who had moved to London, Ontario. The southwestern Ontario landscape was working its strange humid way on me. I felt hung about with sandbags, encumbered and slow and strangely panicky. My circumstances were suddenly so odd to me: I had, for the duration of my visit, become one of a troupe of daughters, and it was a role uniquely unsuited to my sense of privacy. It wasn't because I was not made welcome. On the contrary, my bestie and her two sisters were sweet and accommodating; the youngest gave up her bedroom for me and moved in with her middle sister for the duration of my visit. But I couldn't quite keep up with the pace and culture of that household: they planned group activities and trips and took dozens of photos of the fun we were having. It was so foreign to me: all the money spent, the merrymaking, the bizarre landscape of Ontario Place. A few years later, in grade twelve, I would read "Lord Hamlet is a prince, out of thy star" and recognize it. This trip was princely beyond my star, this family was beyond my star and I was stunningly, sickeningly homesick. And then there was Alice.

Claiming Alice Munro as an early influence is a bit like claiming God as your co-pilot. I know the story that Sheila Munro, in her 2001 memoir, *Lives of Mothers and Daughters: Growing Up With Alice Munro*, tells about the "certain group of well-known Canadian women writers" who allegedly refer to Munro as "the Sublime Alice." I am not well known enough that Sheila Munro would be referring to me, and yet I felt indicted by her pronouncement. Believe me, I know all about praising Munro's skill so unequivocally that there's no room to do anything but agree or pronounce yourself a hater. But where I'm going with this has nothing to do with literary elitism or hero worship.

I was sexually assaulted when I was twelve. After that, it was hard for me to be the kid I was supposed to be, or the young adult I was supposed to grow into, because the assault and the incalculable effort it took for me to be a functioning person afterward made me into an old woman almost immediately. Extreme violence is a time machine. It was hard to listen to my parents because they seemed so naive about the evil that lurked in the world, but I needed their protection for at least six more years, until I was eighteen. The term *PTSD* wasn't in common use at the time, or at least it wasn't in my grade seven class, and in the manner of vicious but useful irony, my slow shuffle through the world looked like adolescent angst to nearly everyone.

The summer I was staying with my bestie's family, her mother gave me a book. I don't know why she did it; probably she just didn't know what to do with me. Or maybe she knew that something had to be done about my sadness. The book was *Dance of the Happy Shades*, and she noted breezily that the author had lived next door to them for a while. Munro moved to London in 1974, commuting first to York University where she taught creative writing before serving as writer-in-residence at London's University of Western Ontario. My bestie's mother was a sophisticate whose girlhood in Montreal marked her as more urban and savvy than the other mothers I knew – though she and my mother were, in a way I can't quite grasp, friends who corresponded for years. She might have read *Dance of the Happy Shades*. Then again, she could have bought a copy of the book because she had met the author over their shared back fence.

Though the word *Happy* in the title made me immediately suspicious, I was hooked by the idea of a writer who had lived next door, and I started reading that night. I read it from cover to cover because I could not quite believe what I was seeing. How could this writer do it? How could she write so evocatively about what I knew intimately but would not say, could not write down and would never detail even in casual conversation with friends: the everyday but completely private world of outdated appliances, clothes that didn't quite fit, money that was enough but never really enough, farmhouses where I'd be sent to the cellar for a jar of beets and hear things (mice? snakes?) moving stealthily. How did Alice Munro see inside my head? The book didn't cure my sadness, though I snapped awake in a whole different way. What the hell was going on in this book about working-class girls that didn't offer moralistic summaries? I remained out of tune with my bestie's home life, but now I was listening to something else: an external voice that was somehow weirdly, unimaginably interior.

These girls in Munro's book were their own selves in a way I hadn't read before. They screwed up and knew humiliation and shame. They were not fake-wise or especially good or innocent, but instead they were solidly real in their puzzlements about being female in an often contemptuous, vicious world. The stories also pointed out aspects of masculinity with which I was already familiar: silent exasperated fathers, aggressive boyfriends, creepy older dudes with their come-ons.

I started staring out of the window of my borrowed bedroom at the house next door, the house where Munro had lived; she was long gone, moved to Clinton, Ontario, but I stared anyway, trying to sync up the stories and the place. I reread *Dance of the Happy Shades* when I got home, and a year later, I had a huge fight with my boyfriend about *Lives of Girls and Women* when he made the mistake of assuming he knew the content from a glance at the cover. I'll never forget his confident know-nothingness and my responding fury. The state of being female was something I had spent most of my life ignoring, but violence had made me acutely aware that be-ing female and ignoring it could kill me. I wasn't much like Munro's bold, young protagonists, and I never set foot in Huron County until 2011. But Munro's psychic landscape was undeniably mine: embar-rassing aunts, sudden violence, ground-down people trapped by their own terrible hope in the capitalist crises of the mid-twentieth century. Munro was at the very start of her career; she would soon be so lauded that it seems faintly ridiculous now to emphasize the influence of those early books. But at the time, I had never read anything like them.

Years later, I returned to academic study, lured by feminist theory, and found that there was an entire course dedicated to Munro's work to be offered that spring. This was like discovering a better quality of oxygen. I registered and reread obsessively before the course began. But my student colleagues were so cavalier; asked why they were taking the course, they shrugged and said it fit their schedule. I was an overachieving ball of class anxiety, and it was clear to me in that moment that my feverish preparations had been excessive. When my turn came to say why I had chosen the course, I did not know how to lie or be casual; I said, "I've been reading Munro for twenty years." I saw the professor's face brighten at the same time as everyone else rolled their eyes.

Everything about Munro – and about me as a reader – is too much: her bazillion awards, her international reputation, the crit-ical footprint made by her many books. My background isn't that different from every female or non-binary artist who has had their lives shaped by violence and its lived contradictions. Reading Munro made me resilient; her observations about injustice and possibility and time allowed me to recognize myself without fear or apology. This took a long time to develop. When I was seven-teen, I thought a lot about Del's insight at the end of *Lives of Girls and Women*: "The future could be furnished without love or scholarships."

I thought of this even when I was surrounded by love and scholar-ships: I knew how quickly things could change.

Munro's early stories feature women and girls who are recogniz-ably classed in their attitudes and embarrassments: always working class, always small town, always aware that there is something they are missing. When I was a younger reader, I liked Munro's girls and young women because they were enraged by mannerisms and expressions the way I was, because they were as suspicious of peo-ple's motives as I was, because they were whole people trapped in the bodies of minors and because they suspected the political truth about female oppression but couldn't quite articulate it, just as I could not. I also liked their rural and small-town roots because I never saw context anywhere else in my life for my family's frequent trips to Boissevain and Margaret and Deloraine and Wawanesa to visit relatives. No one else at school seemed to take these kinds of weekend trips to farms and tiny towns, and have to sit in living rooms and read yellowing farm journals. These were working farms without any of the trappings of farms found in books. I didn't feel more in touch with anything after a visit, contrary to the romantic notions I learned at school about the beauty of being "out in the country."

I also liked the way Munro's young heroines articulated their small revelations without implying that their insight would change their circumstances. I liked how they never hesitated to turn their exacting gazes on older women who acted, by blood or by circum-stance, as guides. Munro's young women weren't sweetly innocent or winsomely philosophical; they possessed exactly no quality that my own mother and aunts would want me to imitate. It is hilarious in retrospect that it was my aunt who gave me that copy of *Lives of Girls and Women* ostensibly because the goopy, sun-drenched cover of the 1971 Signet paperback edition suggested sweetness and fulfilled romance. "Ha!" I thought, "I've already read *Dance of the*

Happy Shades and I am not fooled by this cheap marketing ploy!" It was my secret delight that my aunt had given me such a subversive book and didn't even know it. Or maybe she did.

Stopped at an intersection in Stratford, on the way to see Seana McKenna in *The Matchmaker* in July 2012, my mother in the passenger seat of my car, I watched Alice Munro cross the street in front of us. She leaned on a younger woman's arm; she looked frail, the way my mother was starting to look. I almost didn't say anything, but finally settled for a brief declaration of the miraculous. "That's Alice Munro," I said, with an understated casualness I didn't feel. My mother craned her neck to see. Together we observed Munro's slow progress across the road. I had nothing else to say. My mother had only three years to live, but we didn't know that then. My father had been dead for eight years, and my bestie's mother, who gave me the book, had died of cancer twenty years before. My abuser, the last I heard, is still alive. This is like an ending to a Munro story, except it's clumsy with memory the way her writing never is. I don't want to belabour the point: I'm just not able to leave it as is.

What Sticks When You Are From the Sticks

Fifteen Ways of Looking at Where You Came From

1. Always recognize
2. that most ppl who do community-building
3. in art circles
4. were raised poor
5. & that class is a thing that sticks
   – Jacob McArthur Mooney, tweeted August 29, 2017

The Way You Talk:

I was waiting to start a reading in Winnipeg and sitting with one of the other poets, someone I had met a few times but didn't know well. We were talking when he said, "I can tell where you came from." I sputtered a bit and said I was from Winnipeg, but he went on. "Okay, but I can tell your mother or father came from somewhere in southern Manitoba, near the border, that area." He named towns very close to where my parents had grown up, saying that he had worked for many summers on farms in that area and knew the regional accent. "There's no mistaking it," he said, "I can hear it in your vowels." He then apologized for embarrassing me, though he hadn't. But he had reminded me that I wasn't really class-passing. I felt thoroughly Eliza Doolittled, and was reminded of how in theatre school I was told to change my speech, though I didn't suffer half the cruel criticism received by students from more rural areas, or the jokes levelled at students from outside Canada.

The Way You Keep Talking:

I was in Toronto and on slate for another reading, when at the venue I was introduced to another poet who I knew by reputation. As we shook hands, he pulled me close and said, low but clear in my ear, "I love your accent." I had no idea what I was supposed to make of this: part flirtation, part class marker. I said, "Thank you," because I had no idea what else was required or what else he expected. After my mother died, I found myself phoning my aunt – who was my mother's vocal twin – just to hear her voice whenever she answered the phone. Some days, I think I can hide how much I sound like both of them, but the longer I spend away from the home place, the less I care what anyone thinks of my quasi-rural vowels and hard consonants.

Historically, Canada has taken enormous pride in thinking of itself as a classless society; this is part of our view of ourselves as being more accepting, more liberal, more tolerant than the United States. This is not accurate; as anti-racist activists have been pointing out for decades, though Canada likes to practice its divisiveness in a sometimes though not always subtler fashion than the United States, its class divisions are rigorously upheld. And it's important to maintaining the divisions that they are not really acknowledged – the better to dismiss and sometimes gaslight those who raise questions about Canada's class divisions. But as my Toronto friend's mother demonstrated when she hurried to point out the division between her family and mine, most Canadians have the language to speak about these divisions at their disposal, when they wish it. It's crass to mention class, until you feel that you need to defend you and yours.

This is the book my mother was afraid I would write: about the subtle forms of class shaming and class fear of which she was well aware. She could always manoeuvre around them with her charm, her skills in hosting, her endless imagination for including people.

If she was here, and in a way she is always here, I would say: Mum, it'll be okay. I'm cheesing off all the right people.

Booking It:

My two favourite books about class differences, texts that are both readable and unflinching in their analysis, are not new. Paul Fussell wrote *Class: A Guide Through the American Status System* in 1983, and bell hooks wrote *Where We Stand: Class Matters* in 2000. Fussell's book maintains, among other things, that Americans are as exacting about preserving the divisions in social class as the British, and offers his theory of no fewer than nine separate social classes. Fussell, also author of the excellent and very class-conscious *The Great War and Modern Memory*, was attuned to the nuances of class and status. The verve of his book is his thin slicing of the American class system by examining speech, clothing, hobbies and religious beliefs, making the book a kind of negative primer about the defining characteristic of "taste," which, Fussell notes, is the preferred differentiating term in the United States. The narrative's always-tart delivery targets the kind of snobbery that cares less about actual money and more about style, and the degree to which Fussell's own style sends up taste as the differentiating term between classes makes the book both an entertaining and horrifying read for those of us who grew up aware of the need to class pass. For all its limitations, Fussell's book crackles with eagerness to skewer all of the pretentions of white America, and his note that the middle class is "distinguishable more by its earnestness and psychic insecurity than by its middle income" is bumper-sticker succinct. That said, because it maintains a veneer of a private joke taken to extremes, I can't wholeheartedly recommend Fussell's book to everyone.

A more bracing and more wide-ranging class analysis, bell hooks' *Where We Stand: Class Matters* is different in both tone and scope. In this impassioned, politically rigorous and beautifully written book, hooks takes as her primary principle that we must crack open the resistance to talking about class in North America, and that if we do, it will reveal the fundamental structures of harmful ideologies that are used to disempower, oppress and manipulate so many of us. Throughout *Where We Stand*, hooks is clear that this conversation is as vital as those that every citizen in North America needs to have about race, and she links the history and construction of race in North America as being almost always dependent on a dogged refusal to acknowledge class structures and to discuss possible solidarity between working peoples. She also notes, with a good deal of earned exasperation, that keeping people class-scared causes us to police our own speech about class with the result that we perpetually resist the very solidarity that might empower us. For hooks, conversations about race are incomplete without including conversations about the structures of class, and she warns that as long as these are considered completely separate conversations, we will continue to shame each other with our differences.

Both these books take their socio-cultural contexts from the United Sates, but there's no question that Fussell's central point, that taste is used as a code for class in America, has resonance in Canada. Fussell does not ignore artists; he calls them "X people . . . who belong to a category rather than a class" – a good idea, but not one for which I see much evidence, and perhaps this is where Fussell's book fails for me. In fact, Fussell's classed catch-all, taste, has been used by more than one literary critic in Canada as a measuring stick to determine the parameters and exclusivity of CanLit – that is, who is writing Canadian literature and who is not. This is a bit of a rhetorical trick, as invoking class outright would seem like pure snobbery, and using *taste* or *craft* as belonging to a select group of writers is a common bugaboo, despite the fact that neither *taste* nor *craft* are especially rigorous or useful terms. I use neither when I teach: *taste* is so snobby and *craft* so fussy and subjective. Such terms have, as perhaps their users intend, a paralyzing effect on a lot of beginners who wonder if, maybe, their writing is not to the taste of publishers and readers, that maybe they have not been practicing their craft in a tasteful way. The term *tastemaker* is hilariously egotistic. I can't say it without thinking of George Sanders as Addison DeWitt in *All About Eve*, who never said this, but could have: "I am a tastemaker. I cultivate people's taste. And I'll tell you aaaalllll about Eeeeeeeve." While Fussell does not cover all the bases for a class analysis, I highly recommend his skewering of taste.

In *Where We Stand*, hooks identifies the panic that rises, especially in lower-middle-class white people who are only one job loss away from destitution, whenever discussions of class or status appear to put them on the spot, asking them to identify as either poor or white but not both. The perceived danger of these conversations is inherent in the ways we may see (and be seen), in ways that we might presume we can control but cannot, as hooks makes clear: "The neat binary categories of white and black or male and female are not there when it comes to class. How will they identify the enemy. How will they know who to fear and who to challenge." How, indeed, especially if we have been "carefully taught" to fear otherness as dangerous *and* all forms of solidarity as weakness? These various degrees of being "class-scared," in hooks' terms, include careful negotiations of money and cleanliness and respectability and location and background. And in deeply ironic ways, taste has been manipulated by corporatism, capitalism and colonialism; working-class women can carry knock-off Coach purses, like carrying the poison apple and biting it, too.

Watch Your Sound Bites:

When Hilary Swank won the Oscar for Best Actress for her performance in *Million Dollar Baby* in 2005, she made a class declaration in her acceptance speech: "I'm just a girl from a trailer park who had a dream." The day after the award ceremony was broadcast, I was in an elevator with two women who were discussing the awards, and I heard one accuse Swank of "constructing herself as trailer trash" in order to emphasize the dramatic contrast between her humble origins and her grand achievement. The women in the elevator were not buying it; they scorned Swank's declaration – her class "coming out," as it were – as toadying to the rich, playing poor girl to the expectations of the powerful. The women in the elevator were scornful of Swank's self-construction as working-class girl made good; they rolled their eyes as they spurned her for making such a naive class statement, and suggested with this that she was somehow undeserving of the Academy Award for best actress in a lead role.

In the elevator, I kept quiet. But I thought: "Wow. Never tell people about where you come from."

Such questions of identity are nothing to sneeze at. Where you come from, who made you and how, are often sources of pride, and many artists are adept at laying out their influences, cultural and personal. I love to hear these kinds of talks, or read these essays. It's a pleasure to see those influences brought forward and honoured as part of the creative process; it's also good to see them questioned. Minnie Bruce Pratt's "Identity: Skin Blood Heart," collected in the volume *Yours in Struggle: Three Feminist Perspectives* on *Anti-Semitism and Racism*, is a great example of a personal essay that examines a racist upbringing against coming to an artistic and personal consciousness, and I recommend it.

Not everyone is comfortable talking about their influences, especially if you have been mocked for it or told that your influences are not enough to make you an artist. There was a time in my life that when people asked, "What's your background?" I assumed it was a test that I was about to fail. Really, what could I claim? I gleaned my artistic practice bit by bit, from scraps of courses, my own voluminous but esoteric reading practices, the encouragement of a handful of people and the excoriating criticism of others. That wasn't urbane. And it sure wasn't a sound bite.

Groundwork:

In 2013, when David Gilmour's now-famous dismissal of women's literary work hit the airwaves and social media, I missed the first eight hours of online outrage, refutation and recriminations for the best and most ironic of reasons: because I was working. I was teaching one of those women's texts that Gilmour so summarily dismissed in his remarks. For the record, it was Nalo Hopkinson's *Brown Girl in the Ring*. And not only was I teaching a novel by a Caribbean-Canadian woman, I was also talking to students about their ideas, their literary work, their anxieties, their critical essays and their futures, meeting colleagues about future courses, mulling over proposals for future programs, drafting recommendation letters for former students and anticipating the weekly problems that I would have to solve in order to keep everyone reading and thinking and writing and completing their work – including myself. In short, a regular day on campus. My work was exactly what Gilmour eschewed as "not his thing." I was taken aback by the incipient classism embedded in the sexism of Gilmour's dismissal. I know that doing the hardscrabble work of taking care of students, along with their programs and courses, is what working-class women do for many hours a day in their professional-class jobs.

Lost in the Listicle:

Sometimes I think my class is the first thing people see: as obvious as the nose on my face, or maybe the teeth in my head. My mother used to refer to my teeth as perfect, but that's relative. I have come to the not-unhappy conclusion that they are working-class teeth: a little snaggly, a little crowded, a little bucked. My mouth bears the formative evidence of having a dental plan that covered some things and not others.

A series of listicles made the social media rounds a few years ago that pointed out habits that readers would recognize if they had "grown up poor." The best and most specific of these is "The 5 Stupidest Habits You Develop Growing up Poor," posted by John Cheese on *Cracked* in 2012. I read it with a diagnostic eye: Were these my habits? I feel like I sidestepped some of them, but Cheese caught me on two raised-on-a-budget habits: my preference for canned fruit, and again on the obsessive checking of my bank balance. Busted. How poor were we? Not too poor, and not too well off, either. Maybe the strongest evidence is that I mentally looked over my shoulder as I read that listicle in the privacy of my office; I didn't want to be caught "thinking poor," even as I was acknowledging that I did.

My parents were absolutely forward-thinking people who believed in the modern future, but they were defined, perpetually and it seems happily enough, by their mutual poor white upbringing. When they achieved, they never took it for granted; when they did not achieve, they never took it with bad grace. They were, after all, grateful just to be nominated into this striving.

Always tell people where you come from.

Writing is work, though we are invited to scoff at its version of sweat because, like every white-collar job my father ever heard of, "it beats digging ditches." But I like the way that the phrase *working writer* echoes my working-class background. My luckiest score was that my working-class parents valued the written word. They didn't always understand that if I was reading or in front of a computer screen, I was working, but their own desire to leave the poverty of their rural families and make their way in the small city that seemed huge to them made them rebels of a kind, as well: rebels born out of economic necessity, but rebels nonetheless.

Lost in Modernism:

My mother used to say that she would regularly get lost in her high school because the building was so large and the student body was a dozen times larger than the population of her hometown. She was afraid of the staircase in particular, of how climbing the stairs always seemed to flip the map of the school she tried to carry in her head. This story of getting lost in high school was legendary in our family by the time she pointed out the building to me. I couldn't believe it; we had driven by it hundreds of times. It was not much bigger than my elementary school. *That,* the two-storey brick school like dozens in the neighbourhood and throughout the city, was the huge scary building? After I recovered from the vertigo of seeing her past alongside my present, it became easy to think of my mother, an underfed fourteen-year-old who looked twelve, newly arrived in the city from a town with a population of forty, with her knees knocking together as she approached the building. She knew no one and the city was too overwhelming. She left school as soon as she could, at sixteen, the age at which she was expected to begin earning her keep until she got married.

My mother was not ambitious for herself, but she was ambitious for me, and she did me the extra favour of trusting that I would figure out what reading meant, if it was worth anything. I had a childless aunt who was consistently – and inexplicably – enraged by the sight of me reading. Without fail, she would pipe up in protest, most often saying to my mother, "Get that child's nose out of that book!" To this day, I don't know why this was an offensive sight to her. She was never specific about where else she thought I should be. The kitchen? The laundry room? I never found out largely because my mother took distinct pleasure in not doing what her bossy sister-in-law commanded. So if my mother did have anything to say about it (and she always did), I was left alone to read. These are the sorts of allies that every young artist needs – different from artistic role models or mentors or people who actively show you the way, but often quieter, more subtly subversive people who make the dailiness of practice possible in a young artist's world: time to read, write, walk, think. I know that this gesture, buttressed by my father's dedicated consumption of two books a week, doesn't add up to a life of artistic daring, but context is everything, and so often we forget the context from which we came when we want to shift gears into artistic practice. Either that or we pretend we live perfect lives in art, unsullied by banalities or uncool relatives.

But having parents who supported my endeavours in small ways didn't mean that I wasn't told more than once that people like us didn't get away with anything. My parents feared that I would be crushed by the world, that I would be judged according to my class rather than my abilities, or even that my abilities would not be allowed to increase because I would be denied access to the education, the opportunities, the milieu, the class privilege that would foster them. This was of course all unspoken, as it always is.

Radical Cheek:

I like the "Unlikely Radical" pin I wear several times a year to public events, but only because no one has yet made me an "Unwieldy Radical" pin.

Shortly after my first book was published, a few people took the time to explain to me that I should never speak of myself as a radical, because according to what I had produced in that book, I hadn't a radical bone in my body. I was also told that I should be more urbane, advice I took to heart until it became clear that while people can change, in the end we can only be what we are: a paradox, but a lived one. I tell you this to let you know that people will say discouraging things to you. Even your mentors will be wrong about you, as they sometimes were about me. I am not radical in the way that my critics meant. My aesthetic is not groundbreaking; I'm not changing the language or inventing new forms. Realistically speaking, no one is going to point to a form I've invented and make a Wikipedia entry about it.

But in the day-to-day, gotta-buy-groceries world, very few people are radical in that way, and I can now look at that criticism with some realism. Not every scientist discovers a new element. Not every athlete breaks a world record. But it is foolish to suggest that people should not study chemistry or train for a marathon because they will not make history. So, too, with an artistic practice, and if you're an out-of-liner, you know that radicalism is relative. Whenever and wherever I teach poetry or talk about its value in the world, whenever I read it aloud – my own or other people's poems – I feel as radical as though I am growing antlers. And people often look at me that way when I talk about or read poetry out loud, in public, where anyone can hear me; they are sometimes horrified, sometimes curious, sometimes happy. I have worked and lived and written and performed in plenty of places where naming reality is as radical as it gets, and there I've been pretty dangerous. I've also been to plenty of other places where a more radical view was absolutely necessary, and in those places I was not especially out on a limb.

When I was a young artist, there was a popular and profoundly misused theory of training that students had to be "broken down" so they could be built back up into their artistic self. This is ridiculous and often cruel. I saw people broken and it was in no way a good thing. There's no denying that discovering your artistic self is a profound change, but change has to be accompanied by choice. That doesn't mean that you shouldn't study the greats, or read voraciously, or learn new methods, or invest your time in trying new approaches. Change is good when change means more tools, more ideas: you can still be you and learn from Emily Dickinson or Oscar Wilde, or study cubism or improv or political science. It's a big world even if your place in it is small.

I think my early critics were disturbed by my lack of embarrassment about my class background. I remember giving a presentation in class in which I did not use every academic term perfectly; why shouldn't I (and everyone else) be allowed moments when we stop and make sure we are using the terms of a new discourse correctly? Is it not urbane to ask for correction or guidance? My critic's comment at the time was self-serving in a way; they wanted me to impress them in a particular way that didn't make sense to me. They wanted me to demonstrate daring and risk according to their standards. What that person didn't get about me was that I had been out there on the small branches – far, far out of a safe context – and being risky for many years. Radical is also relational.

Too Big for Your Bootstrapping:

In *Lament for a Nation*, George Grant called the United States of America "the great liberal experiment to the south," and while he had other names for Canada, I wonder if we could call Canada the great status experiment to the north. Our delusion that this society is classless means denying huge chunks of history and turning our faces from the ways that the nation-state has treated BIPOC people and anyone other than the bone-white middle and upper classes as though they are not quite good enough citizens. But while the "classless society" of Canada remains a moderately popular myth among the upper-middle class, I strongly suspect that everyone else, from the rich to the working poor, knows it is bunk. The working class and their close counterparts, the striving lower-middle class, experience class markers every day, but are kept, mostly, from commenting on them because to do so would draw attention to their own class position. Keeping people class-scared, to use hooks' term, calcifies us, not necessarily freezing us out of mobility potential but often shutting down discourse about class backgrounds. As hooks notes, our inability or unwillingness to speak to the distinction between classes is a self-perpetuating system of estrangement. Throughout the middle decades of the twentieth century, and stretching into the 1967 Centennial celebrations and beyond, Canada was very effective in cultivating middlebrow culture as a desirable class camouflage for those, like my parents, who found themselves with increased opportunities for class mobility after World War II.

American culture loves a Horatio Alger story, a rags-to-riches trope that has contributed significantly to a damaging narrative of bootstrapping and the resultant blaming of low-income earners for their own circumstances. Mainstream Canadian culture, not too differently, loves to narrativize a working-class background to boast about the Prairies as the breadbasket of the world, about our economic recovery after the Great Depression, about Canada as a young country rich in renewable resources and other greatest hits of Canadian nationalism.

But in university, whether you are a student or a professor, you will be asked – and sometimes required – to use forms of speech and writing that are antithetical to your upbringing and class-consciousness. This can have some very estranging results, especially if you feel as though you are being required to deny or muffle your background, or even to perform your working-class values as an example of the benevolence and accessibility of the system. To attend university – or any kind of classes that indicate educational advancement – can also be seen as a class betrayal, a declaration that you are now too good for your own background, or in my parents' words, "too big for your boots." Becoming a working artist might mean weathering accusations of snobbiness or pretension, and any foray into the wider world undertaken on behalf of an artistic practice, curiosity or nurturance can connote class betrayal, even if the move is temporary. The class betrayal can even take place without the young artist leaving their hometown, or even the family home, if the artistic exploration takes time away from what the family sees as necessary work or more appropriate pursuits. Paint all you want; a quarter-section waits for no one. As poet Pearl Pirie puts it when referencing her working-class upbringing, "Expertise was defined as bullshitting pride. No one knows nothing about anything. To say so is to be uppity and compete with God: to invite being struck down. Poverty, class, Christianity, Buddhism and cynical poets have overlapping Venn circles in this." But Pirie also makes it clear that the good news about coming to art from a working-class background is that it burns away pretention: "I just was an artist. There's no Making It, just making things. Anyone can opt in."

Look for Your Sisters:
In Canadian literature, it is not hard to find the "working-class hero," and he is inevitably male: gritty and hard-nosed, admired for his ambition, his refusal of cultural and social norms. He may be a character (in a novel by David Adams Richards or Frederick Philip Grove) or an author himself (Al Purdy, Milton Acorn, Richards again). True to bell hooks' warning that gender binaries reinforce resistance to discussions of race, the working-class woman remains

– half a century after Alice Munro won the Governor General's Award for *Dance of the Happy Shades* – a highly negotiated figure, in print and in real life, despite the fact that working-class women are everywhere in the pages of Canadian literature. While Munro and Purdy both rose to prominence in the late 1960s and went on to have extended literary careers, Purdy was allowed to pen poems containing lines like "Keep your ass outta my beer!" while Munro remained constantly under scrutiny, a curiosity whose talent was undeniable but whose background was often discussed – like Shakespeare's – as impossible to support her skill.

But what if these working-class women are your mother, your aunts, your sisters and cousins, your father's unmarried cousin who lived on the farm until she was ninety-two, your grandmothers? To me, these women are entirely imaginable because despite my class mobility, I am still inevitably one of them. It's not like a skin you can shed. I was glad to find, in my reading as a grad student, Margaret Laurence and Adele Wiseman and Gabrielle Roy and Lee Maracle and Lynn Coady and SKY Lee and Dionne Brand and many other women writers saying, in their books, here, *here* are working women's lives – right here, where you knew they were all along.

We can only be who we are. And we can be who we are as much, and as well, as we can.

Work, but Not Harder:

My parents' deaths have left me thinking a lot about my upbringing and class, in ways that I managed to gloss over in my rush to achieve. As I continue to gain status, recent conversations about the abuse of male and white privilege in the academy and in the writing community have brought me to the attention of disgruntled men whose long-held privilege is now being questioned. Let me tell you, friendly in your ear, there is nothing quite like being a working-class woman who stopped writing poetry for a few years in order to train new writers in literary citizenship and the politics of making meaning, and having a white upper-class man rage at you because you are not teaching his book in your courses or promoting his project.

I don't write fiction because real life is strange enough.

Recent conversations about white privilege have also thrown my working-class background into sharp relief, reminding me that we all exist on a continuum of privilege. It is important to pay attention to inequities and injustices, and to think about the kinds of solidarities we can establish between ourselves when we speak our realities. The poet and performance artist (and my former student) Janice Lee made stickers quoting Flavia Dzodan's 2011 declaration "My feminism will be intersectional or it will be bullshit," which says it all. I am crediting Janice as well as Dzodan here, as it was through Janice that I discovered that phrase. Sometimes your students and former students bring you great things and you need to thank them, publicly.

My feminism has not always been as intersectional as it could be, so in an effort to have it be meaningful and not bullshit, I too am working on doing things differently. The corporatization of the academy has re-exposed class markers with the finger-wagging insistence that everyone "must work harder" (an absolutely unironic reference to *Animal Farm*). It has also played upon the anxieties of everyone who does not fit the traditional idea of a professor, as it suggests that we have been allowed into the academy on sufferance and must be forever, demonstrably, grateful for the chance. This is particularly true of those of us who have been vocal about ways that the institution reinforces class by asking us to do more with less. Are you kidding? Working-class women know how to make a four-course meal out of dust. Of course I know how to do with less. But while I am doing more with less, who else is making no changes at all?

Never Tell Anyone You Waited Tables:

Once, long ago, my first book was a finalist for an award. This was a biggish deal as these things go, and it was certainly the first time anything I had written had received national recognition. When the nomination announcement was released alongside blurbs from the judges, I was gobsmacked. Every other book was glossed with phrases like "a bold new aesthetic" or "innovation in poetry" and other lush praise. It was puzzling. I thought, "How can they all offer a bold new aesthetic?" The fifth blurb was about my book and included the phrase "interesting poems about waitressing." For the record, there were exactly two poems about restaurant work in that book. I don't know who wrote that assessment and I am pretty sure that I don't want to know. More bafflingly, now that I have sat on such committees myself, I don't know how the chair of the committee could have looked over these five blurbs and approved them for the press release. I can only assume that someone was asleep at the switch, because the alternative is that they thought the shortlisted books merited exactly this kind of class comparison.

Welcome to the new world; looks like the old world.

What Sticks:

People who were raised working class or striving class have a different view of "working for free," as one does in arts communities – sometimes for one's own benefit, or more often for the good of the community. "Working for free" is fine when working for a defined, observable community with perceivable and measurable systems of give and take in place. It becomes a lot less fine when the community is a concept without definable boundaries or systems of reciprocity, when the people doing the work are indifferently (or never) compensated. It becomes an even bigger problem when the "community" supports only those who are always supported:

usually well-known people with, relatively speaking, opportunities galore. Real community work is not theoretical to anyone who has lived and worked in a small community that relies on the sweat equity and resourcefulness of its members. In fact, I note that in the circles I was raised, the word *community* was rarely used – except in the case of *community centre* – because community work was implicitly necessary. My parents were old hands at this. They worked around and through a stream of never-ending tasks: took in other people's kids at a moment's notice, coached baseball, took old people for groceries, shovelled snow from walks and driveways, fed the hungry, donated stuff, baked stuff, loaned stuff, pushed cars out of snowbanks. I do not mean to make this sound idyllic: it was nothing fancy.

Are you working to get things up and running? Or are you working for the concept of community, not helping out people you know because they would (and will) do the same for you but to support an external view of "community" as a commodity? What sticks in your creative community? People who have been raised striving class are no strangers to hard work. We often make excellent artists and community contributors because our expectations of what a job entails, or what is reasonable compensation for effort, fall outside of the capitalist system. This also means that we are sometimes taken advantage of, treated badly and treated as though we work for peers who partake of our generosity and hard work.

Speak of Such Things:

When I first read Heather Milne's interview with Sina Queyras in *Prismatic Publics*, I had that feeling of hearing an open secret spoken aloud. When asked about how she was reading the trajectories of two other poets, Sina said, "Well, I'm a working-class girl. [Bronwen] Wallace and [Erín] Moure are working-class girls." This was a thing I knew but wasn't yet saying about myself, about the writers whose work I loved and researched and wrote about, mostly because I had learned as a doctoral student that such admissions make female professors especially vulnerable to accusations of not being professional, and women writers vulnerable to accusations of "not understanding" the works of "great men." To be honest, I laugh every time I read that phrase and yet it persists like a bad smell.

Once I left Winnipeg, where many people had rural backgrounds a generation or two back, and where it was easy to feel the lingering ghost of the Winnipeg General Strike almost a century later, I was ideologically shamed out of discussing class.

A real scholar, and a real writer, doesn't speak of such things.

Ah, but we do.

The Empress has No Clothes:

Is it because when she was young, her family couldn't afford shoes? Or is it because she has thrown off your lendings?

Always let them know where you come from.

Envy and the Long Game

While it would be wrong to say that I have figured out everything about my own class mobility, including my (debatable) transition to professional class and what effects that has had on my artistic production, it has occurred to me that being grateful for the opportunity to work yourself to death means something very different for me in 2018 than it did for my Depression-reared parents in the mid-1950s. Definitions of work change over generations, something of which I feel very aware as I teach students who identify as millennials, or alternatively, as people who resist that label and the cruel characterizations that can accompany it. How then do envy and scorn work in artistic communities, and how, as beginner artists and thinking mentors, might we meet some of these challenges for the good of our own working lives, and for that of our communities? There can be no denying that there is sometimes envy between artists. People can be envious of opportunities that come to one person in a community, via excellent work or extra effort or sometimes mere happenstance, as well as chances that one person's money and position make possible. The list can be pretty long and chance plays a part much of the time, because of one person's gift of the gab or gregarious personality, or because someone else has a poem in the right issue of the right literary journal at the right time to catch an influential editor's eye. The circumstances can be complex, but the emotions are bluntly direct.

Susan Fiske's 2011 study *Envy Up, Scorn Down* uses the core terms of *envy* and *scorn* to emphasize divisions of class based on affect or feeling. Fiske points out that as our status rises we become the subject of envy, and if we believe our own press (including our own social media feeds), we are made more susceptible to scorning those who do not seem to have what we have: privilege, money, status, experience, etc. Envy rises like hot air, while scorn falls like a lead weight. I wonder, too, about the many ways in which frequent traversing of the area between scorn and envy in arts communities – up and down that slope, as Fiske suggests – might muddy the ground enough so that scorn and envy could be mistaken for one another.

The most profound envy of all in most arts communities is the envy of artists who have more time to make art than you do. This is, for many writers and artists, the ultimate luxury: not having to work at a day job for a forty- to fifty-hour week and then try to practice their art in their "spare time." My own core of envy is fairly obsessed with time. For years, I have heard writing colleagues speak lovingly, caressingly, of having time to write. I have heard the parents of very young children talk the same covetous way about sleep. At any artists' residency (itself a huge privilege and luxury), you can hear people sigh blissfully as the artists describe what it is like to have time to write (and we stretch those vowels out, too: tiiiiime to wriiiiiite) every day for a week or two. You can hear their soul-shivering, quasi-erotic vocalization of the experience of having time. I've done it, too. This is not my scorn talking; it is my envy.

But there are exceptions to how even this most envied commodity is regarded. The last time I was at the Banff Centre for an academic conference, a few of us wound up sharing a lunch table with writer and all-around Canadian Renaissance woman Mary Walsh, who was there finishing her novel *Crying for the Moon*. She said to us, incredulously, "I've taken four years to write this novel! Can you believe it?" The three of us sitting at the table with her, all academics with books that had taken years to write, blinked in surprise. We all knew that Walsh wasn't writing the novel full-time or anything like it. She was fitting it in – as we all do – with her other paying gigs. It's true that most of us don't have paying gigs like Mary Walsh does: being Marg, Princess Warrior, as well as writing comedy sketches for *This Hour has 22 Minutes*, her own TV shows and a ton of side projects. But like anything else, these money-earning projects ate the time she wanted to spend working on her novel. As over-employed women ourselves, my colleagues and I assured Walsh that she wasn't taking too long. "Four years isn't a lot of time for a novel," we said. "Some might consider it a blistering pace, all things considered." Walsh laughed and said, "Well, I'm used to writing a comedy sketch in thirty minutes, so that's my standard." She sounded exactly like every woman in my family; that's a working-class woman talking. Time is money.

Envy of another's chances or successes can run deep, and the poisonous potency of that envy can ruin a community. Fiske writes about scorning "downwards," toward those less privileged than oneself, but I would argue that we can and do scorn "upwards," too. I'm not immune; remember the chip on my shoulder as I entered my first poetry workshop? My fear was running me, and in the grip of it, I scorned everyone in the room before I had even met them. I am exhausted just remembering it. Scorn and envy take a lot out of you. Scorn can also get bundled with envy in a big ball of bitterness when one person in a cohort is a risk-taker, or leverages their privilege and achieves something before the others do. One man in the first poetry workshop I took published before all the rest of us did. He couldn't have been less pretentious about it; his attitude was that he was a bit surprised himself, and grateful for the chance. He was not egotistic and he did not flaunt his success; he was just grateful and happy. I remember watching him talking about his good luck in class, and in my envy I allowed myself some grandiose thoughts. I recall thinking that he had it all handled. He wasn't inching along like the rest of us; he was set. I could see the book he would publish while I worked my day job without respite or publication. And then I would die. In a ditch. Unloved.

This is exactly as ridiculous as it sounds. He had published one piece and my envy was way out of proportion. That is the scope of envy; it is by definition a monster. A more logical and productive outlook, one I recommend as daily practice, is followed by many smart artists: a belief in the propinquity of success. If the person next to you scores, that is evidence that you can and will soon. You are next. Instead of thinking that lightning never strikes in the same place twice, remember that when it rains, everyone gets wet.

Scorn is a bit different and can be particularly vehement between classes, especially if you are someone who hovers on that knife-edge of class-passing. Fiske notes that each of us wants to be in the upward position: morally or righteously, if not due to our status, class or privilege. I wish I could honestly tell you that I rise above the scorn every time, but I tend to scorn when I am scorned. When I am on the receiving end of scorn, and someone takes the position that they are rolling a ball of disdain downhill toward me, my reaction is that it is impossible. Indeed, I assert, I am uphill from *them* and rolling disdain downhill toward them. This is asinine behaviour that I indulge in less and less as I get older, but I can't pretend that this hasn't happened.

*

When I wrote that this book is the book my mother was afraid I would write, I meant that I am flying in the face of decades of careful class-passing. But negative capability is a real force in the world, and my mother's hard work gave me the handholds and footholds to climb the wall, to get to the university and their library where I learned that writers could come from Canada, and further and wilder, that some of them were women and some of them wrote about things that were like my life. I also learned that you could go places and train to be an actor, a writer, an artist. Then I met people who did that and had to think about the differences between us, and eventually I came to the conclusion that the differences were manageable.

Being class-scared is a tough code to live by, to strain against, to bear up under the ostentatious display of wealth in the western world. The '80s, that era of conspicuous consumption, was my personal era of conspicuous thriftiness, living on a shoestring with an up-and-down savings account and plenty of real-life practical knowledge about how to live on very little. Decades later, I think of all that hard work – my parents' and my own – and I'm tired of pretending that class and the work of class-passing doesn't occupy a significant chunk of my brain. I'm tired of the charade that reinforces the myth that everything for which I've worked like a dog came naturally; I'm tired of tidying away my effort. The only reason I can address any of this in the first place is because I have reached a particular position in professional middle-class stability, much as I still chafe against it. From here, my osprey's nest of class mobility, I will say what I see.

Travel is one of those privileges. I cannot count the number of times I have zoned out at parties or dinners at the homes of friends when the conversation has turned to where people travelled this year, because I still don't take big trips in anything resembling a cavalier manner. I didn't grow up with exotic vacations or trips to cosmopolitan cities, so I felt an instant kinship when Brenda Schmidt wrote: "In my forties I made my one and only trip to Europe with a friend. Up until that point I'd felt self-conscious and embarrassed at writing retreats when during happy hour other writers launched into conversations about their worldly travels. Nothing, I repeat nothing, made me feel more like I didn't belong than those wine-swirling happy hour travel conversations." I hear you, sister.

Our vacations when I was young meant packing up the car, piling in, driving for a few hours and setting up the campsite by a lake or river, sometimes in a provincial park, sometimes just in a good spot by a lake. When the campsite set-up was finished, my father would open a lawn chair, sit down by the campfire, open his book and say with a satisfied sigh, "I wonder what the poor people are doing?" It would take me years to understand the irony of that statement, and to be truthful, I am not sure I have gotten to the end of those ironic layers yet.

On the one hand, my dad was asserting that in our no-frills camping (no electricity, no running water), we were rich in other things: fresh air, natural setting, quiet, a chance to get away. On the other hand, I wondered if he was separating himself from the "poor" family in which he was raised, if he was now middle class enough to set himself above it, or if it was a more ironic performance than that: the still-poor mimicking the rich by commenting on the nature and structure of pleasure. And I also know that if I were to have said anything like this to my father, he would have shaken his head: not in disagreement, but indicating confusion, as he often did when he didn't understand what I was saying.

The difficulties of being class-scared are many, but the constant refusal to acknowledge class fear is perhaps the most insidious. Sometimes I can spot someone who grew up like I did, on the leading edge of the striving class, and I know that being spotted is either that person's greatest fear or their greatest wish. I can't claim some magic ability; sometimes I can spot a fellow class-passer, but not always. We are all pretty good at transmuting our fear of discovery into other distracting behaviours. Disturbingly, Paul Fussell in *Class* notes that addiction is a go-to position for people who spend years class-passing. This seems right to me in some ways: the need for external substances to relieve yourself of tension, of the constant wearing of the mask. But at the same time, it seems that some class-passing people avoid drugs and alcohol assiduously and for just the same reason: fear of having the mask slip under a state of induced relaxation. People can make art for similar kinds of reasons; most of the arts offer a chance to both mask and reveal yourself simultaneously.

A belief in the scarcity of resources can make artists bitter if they believe that they can *only* be great *if* they receive this opportunity or that funding. This is given traction in artistic communities that favour a certain style of work or a limited (or restricted) membership. This can be an advantage for out-of-liners who are starting from scratch. If there are not many artists in your community, being as inclusive as possible makes the best sense. Of course, being as inclusive as possible always makes the best sense, but the benefits of being so are wildly obvious if your artistic community is small.

A profound belief in scarcity can be addictive, and our consumer-capitalist culture will supply you with no shortage of reasons to buy into that belief. Some opportunities are by definition scarce (like literary prizes and big publishing contracts), and virtue and hard work are often touted as their own rewards because sometimes artists might feel like that is all we've got. Even small amounts of recognition and a cheque for a bit of money can seem like lifelines if you've been working in obscurity for a long time. For writers, there is no getting around the fact that books take a long time to produce and that we live piecemeal through small pieces of production in those in-between times, which is most of the time. However, allowing your practice to be run primarily by yearning after a big prize, a big break, the promise of "stardom," is the fastest path to frustration. Being ambitious is good and can give you drive, but remember always that art is a Long Game.

How to Stage a Process Installation

Beginner artists are interested in process for very good reasons. After you have been told a few times that you are doing it, you might have a follow-up question: Am I doing it right? How can I do it better? The more you work on a piece of writing, and the more you learn to talk to other writers, the greater your curiosity about how another writer manages to produce work that is so different from yours in style, tone or form. If you are reading widely and run across work that both pleases and mystifies you, you will probably ask yourself, "How did the writer *do* that?"

It is unfortunate that so many experienced artists speak very little about their process, and are sometimes quite secretive, but I understand why. Sometimes a creative process is very hard to explain, especially to someone new to the practice. Yet when I started teaching beginner writers, it became clear that they were starved for a close-up look at practice in-process, and I started using what I called a "process installation" approach to explaining it. I would not have done it had my students not spoken up. In fact, the first few times I taught a poetry course, I avoided using any of my own poetry for what I thought were good reasons. Time with the students was precious and short, and I felt strongly that it should be spent on discussing a broad spectrum of poems and styles, demonstrating tools and techniques, and workshopping students' drafts. Exactly where would my own poetry fit into such a packed schedule?

But then, at the end-of-term literary event with the students to commemorate their completion of the course, I used my five minutes at the microphone to thank them for their hard work, and to read two short poems of mine: one a lyric piece of gratitude, and the second poem a splashy ninety-second performance piece that I had done many times. One of the students said, as she was leaving, that my reading was illuminating for her and that she was disappointed I hadn't read more of my poetry throughout the course. I responded that their poetry should be emphasized, but she was having none of that and replied, "But we want to know what you are writing. We want to know how you are doing it."

I was surprised. After all, I had shown them a list of the tasks I had completed in a long and complicated document called "My Year in Poetry": a chronological listing of every submission, rejection, publication, interview, review, event organization and reading I had given for a year. I had thought that this would exhaust their appetite for real-world evidence of the day-to-day work of poetry. When my student said that she wanted more of my poetry, I was flummoxed until I remembered being a student and trying to figure out how acting worked. It had mattered to me then that I heard how my instructor's day went on a commercial shoot or in a play rehearsal – that no detail was too small for me to turn over and over in my mind as part of my hazy future: what he ate, how many hours he worked, his subway ride to the location were all grist for the mill of how to be an artist. It did not matter that the details were mundane, or even meaningless. Because when everything is a mystery, anything can be a clue. It is up to the instructor to leave some decent clues.

So I took her comments to heart and started planning how I could offer more to help break down the mystery. When I next taught the course, I deliberately drafted a new poem over a ten-day period right in the middle of the teaching term; I wanted this to be fresh. I kept all my stalled starts and bad beginnings, clustered there on the page, teeming. I kept my angst-ridden abstractions and images that went nowhere. I kept saving drafts, kept refining. I worked quickly on the poem, and produced several drafts over the ten-day period. Developing several drafts over a few days is not necessarily an indication of a poem's success. But if I can sit down to look at the draft and am dissatisfied with it while getting decent ideas about how to revise it, that's a good situation for the poem's development, interspersed as it always is with other writing, administrative duties, grading and life stuff. I drew on my many years of experience in workshopping with peers, especially drawing on that day before a workshop when I knew several pairs of eyes would be on the poem, and that I had better stop playing around with the draft and, as the expression goes, bring it.

I brought the draft – my sixth of that poem – to class as part of our lesson for that week: revision process and techniques. I had prepped the students with strategies and lists of revision techniques, which they had been working with on their own pieces and those of their peers, so they weren't newbies to the feedback process. But I was about to ramp up the demonstration level of the course. The students' brows were furrowed as I powered up the projector and told them that I was going to walk them through a number of steps to building a poem, using a poem of my own to do it. This itself was not unusual; I had given them a glimpse of my process earlier in the course, when I had used my sestina "Whiskey Canyon" to talk about the use of form, but had only spent a few minutes on that before moving to other examples of villanelles and sonnets. I started to talk and the brows did not unfurrow: in fact, the furrows deepened. People frowned at the screen like they were born to frown, like it was their calling, like they were getting paid a good union wage to frown. "Tough crowd," I thought, and kept on. A furrowed brow can mean a lot of things. I furrow a lot when I am thinking. A little consternation can be good, and an instructor has to trust her material.

In this case, my material really was *my* material. The poem I had drafted was an elegy, one in a series that I had drafted after my mother's death. My grief was not fresh; it had moved into a constant throb. I had already been through a month-long elegy-writing immersion and felt neither reconciled nor consoled, but practiced. This affective space was my space and I would take up all that was necessary. I am rarely satisfied with elegies, which is probably why I keep writing them. My idea was to show my drafts and discuss a bit, and then keep them up on screen and let the students take their time, discuss, take questions and post the whole snarly imperfect document to the class website so they could peruse it afterwards if they wanted. On the screen, bigger than life, was my tool to unpack the mystery box, undo the anxious knots: my incredibly banal, super-prosey, going-nowhere-and-doing-it-slowly first draft, looking nothing like a poem.

I invited the students into the process, to walk around and look at how the poem developed: the "installation" piece of the "process installation." As a parallel, picture a visual artist's studio with several versions of a sculpture on display: from preliminary sketches to detailed drawings to scaled renderings to plaster casts and, finally, to different sizes and shapes and coloured versions of the sculpture, with one arm, four arms, variously draped with cloth, or paper streamers, or turning on a lathe. One object, multiple stages, simultaneous versions.

I began: "Here's my first draft, my very first lines that I wrote thinking something could be in them." I left a long pause while students gazed at the screen; I let them have a really good look, then said, "You might notice that it's bad. It's like a teenage diary entry, one that you hide. It's prosey, it relies on concepts like pain and sadness and loneliness. This was all true in the moment that I wrote it, but seconds after, I was dissatisfied. The language isn't doing anything. But it has one advantage over the blank page." They waited. I think they could not imagine the advantage, so I broke the silence.

"It's over. It's done. I've broken the seal of the page. I've put an object – a phrase – in the space and now the pressure's off. So now I have a bar to jump over, a bar made from these crappy six lines. Here are six better lines, and those became ten better lines. Then I found a stronger image to focus on. And then I had another idea..." and so it went. I talked the students through the process of drafting the poem, explaining how and why I developed some parts and let others fall away. There was no way I could explain every choice I made, but I discussed what I could and gave them room and time to see what there was to see, and to ask questions. I tried not to rush. No archive can explain everything, but people learn to see things given enough time in the room.

The poem is called "The Haunting," and I showed them that I didn't decide on that title until the fifth draft. I also shared that I spent the first three drafts cramming the poem full of all kinds of extraneous material that I ended up getting rid of in drafts four and five, and that I retained one of the odd images that seemed like a frivolous decision of a moment but grew to deserve its spot in the poem. A fanciful mental side trip into the Paris Catacombs from the most everyday space of my early morning kitchen became a major part of the poem because I took my own frivolity seriously. I showed them how I developed the journey among ancient skulls and femurs as an important way of imagining *l'empire de la mort* as a destination.

Even writing the French phrases – in a language that I have spoken off and on, badly and a bit better, since I was eight – changed how I thought. It loosened up my thinking and reminded me to be expansive in the first few drafts. As I walked them through the drafts, they saw the poem's growth from eight bad lines to fourteen better ones, to thirty lines that started to have some shape, and eventually to a two-page, three-section poem.

Brows stayed furrowed, though I saw some students starting to nod as they traced the pieces of the poem throughout the various drafts. The poem as a poem was not knocking people's socks off, but that was not the goal. It was more important that people started to follow along with some of the choices well enough that they asked questions about the shifts and revisions: Why was the shift to the catacombs important other than its location as a burial site? Was it doing any other work in the poem? Was the rabbit intended as an image of reincarnation? If so, why was it in the first stanza? These were excellent questions.

I understand that writers are protective of their processes. We do not want our ways of writing dissected or picked over or mocked. I was showing the students the hidden side of writing: a decidedly undramatic side that is cluttered with banalities, misfires, metaphors developed with hope then discarded as false leads, odd coincidences that gel into lines and instinctive leaps between drafts. It was a series of images of my brain in action. This was in no way the only way to write, but it was the way I had done it that week and with this particular poem. A version of myself appeared and disappeared several times throughout the drafts as I worked on different perspectives, and my beginner writers asked about this, too: Should the elegist be in the poem or not? How much? Why? I had big concerns at work in the poem that I was not sure I had addressed yet, especially the thinly veiled misogyny of the rituals surrounding a woman's death. In such a case, what were the benefits of having the lyric I as a presence in the poem? I said all that to the students, too, because there was no point in letting them in on the process if I did not admit to my own questions about the unfinished aspects of the poem.

I thought of this exercise as a spatial one, and noted that all of my analogies for it – a map, an installation, a room, an archive – relied on thinking about the poem as a constructed space that required time and the willingness to observe and value stages of the work. I pointed out the topography of the drafts – choices about stanza length here, a developing repetition there – and asked them to note that each draft held a significant series of changes, not just the substitution of a word or an added line. We worked through five drafts together and then I distributed paper copies of the sixth draft. I told them that it was their turn. I had been providing feedback on their poems by marking them up and returning them every week with concrete suggestions for taking them further, and now they would get to do that with my draft. They had already done this with each other, in pairs and small groups. This was different, though: I was the instructor. This was a delicate moment, because I could not pretend that there was not a power differential between us, and that my students might feel reluctant to criticize my work.

So there were several options and a fail-safe. They didn't have to complete this portion if they didn't wish to: no marks, participatory or otherwise, were associated with doing it. Or they could do it and not sign their name to it. Or they could do it, limit themselves to positive comments, and choose between signing and not signing. I told them that I needed assistance to complete the poem, that their eyes were the first on it. I talked about literary communities and reciprocity and the challenge of criticizing senior writers. And maybe most importantly, I told them a story about the first time I was asked to criticize a professor's writing. I was part of a designedly interactive fourth-year seminar in which the professor taught us a handful of major poems from a chosen writer, then gave us his draft of an article he was writing about those poems. He told us that he expected real criticism, that he respected our opinions as writers and that he genuinely wanted our feedback. We took him at his word and went away and furiously marked up his paper copies, and then returned them to the professor who had encouraged us to criticize him. We spent a portion of the next class going over how he could improve the article. I had a few things to say, but wow! My student colleagues were fantastic editors. They really impressed me with their insights and incisiveness, and I wasn't the only one who was impressed. Weeks later, the professor told me that he was shocked to discover how much we had to say; it had been many years since his work had come under such close scrutiny and the ten of us really raked him over the coals. He also said that we shook him awake and thus he revised with new fervour. We are all thanked in the book he wrote later.

I told my students that our situation was slightly different, and actually, more to their advantage: that I had been modelling the feedback method for them for weeks, and that they should apply what they had observed to my poem. I reminded them that I am a veteran of twenty years of workshops in which my peers regularly say things about my work like "That last stanza is extraneous" and "This needs a tough-love revision" and "This is a bit of a mess." I am a human being and it is still possible to offend me, but unless they wrote "What is this crap?" on every line, the chances that they would wound me were pretty slim. I also noted that if they had been feeling a little frustrated that I always had so much to say about their poems yet they never got to see my work, here was their chance to chime in, to say what was working and what was not: to suggest that I revise, go further, reconsider my word choice.

They did it, right in class. They wrote like they were jet-fuelled, much the same way as I revised my professor's work when I was given the chance. It was great. I collected the marked-up copies, thanked them for their work and dismissed the class. Up until then, I had been doing most of the talking. The students had been observing or writing most of this time. Some had asked questions or offered comments, but it had been a pretty busy hour of brainwork: lots of look at, listen to, add up, navigate through, write. I did not expect that they would be so ready to discuss in depth. I had, in fact, designed the feedback writing especially to give them a chance to have their say without the pressure of having to speak aloud. As far as the larger lessons of the revision demonstration were concerned, I was happy with the attention they had paid it, and was just going to let the students absorb the lesson as they wished: now, later or never as they chose.

But a few students hung back in the classroom as the others packed up and left. One knew me well from other courses. She said, "I've never seen anything like that before. I feel a little drunk!" One was a senior student who had already taught quite a bit and had a strong understanding of pedagogy; she thanked me seriously for the intricate lesson, and her thanks showed her understanding of the steps involved in developing the exercise. Although I had not planned beyond this stage, it was clear as soon as I saw the feedback sheets that the exercise was not yet over. There was more work we could do. It is usual for members of a group to disagree on the strengths and weaknesses of a piece, and in a workshop course these disagreements create lively and sometimes heated discussion. But in my courses, as beginner courses with large memberships, students work in small groups of four; while I can hear spikes of dissent among such groups, in general people are more conciliatory than confrontational. But the written feedback was different; it gave me five or six classic examples of conflicting advice. Five people circled a phrase and wrote "this is my favourite image in the poem!" while five others circled the same passage and wrote "cut this." My all-time favourite disagreement was about stanza length: "I love how the stanzas reduce from five lines to three to two," versus "this reduction of stanzas seems overly manipulative." More than one student picked up my feedback phraseology and used it with impunity; notes saying, "suggested cut" and "I don't think this line is doing the work you'd like it to do" littered the pages. And they were right. This was revision-lesson gold, and it was too good to keep to myself.

I contacted my online writing group, the poets of the Electronic Garret, on the basis that they never let me get away with anything. I asked for volunteers to do the same exercise with the same poem: line-by-line written feedback on what worked and what didn't, which would be anonymized and compiled with the students' feedback so that the students could see their own comments alongside that of more experienced poets. Six poets responded, and I created a final feedback copy of the poem with everyone's comments on it. I kept the students' comments under PS for Poetry Students; when there was a schism between students about a piece of the poem, I used the notation PS1 or PS2 as needed. Garretians' comments were recorded with an initial derived from their first names, though the students never knew their names. When I put the sixth draft up on the screen the next week, the lines fairly bristled with feedback. The students waded through it, noting alignment of their own comments with those of the senior poets and the triumph of "getting it right" – though I pointed out to them that the senior poets also made comments that went against the grain of the general feedback, like one poet's cranky question – "What is this rabbit doing here?" about an image that many students had liked, and the blunt criticism of my diction from another poet: "I'm sick of the word apocalypse."

Finally, I showed the students the most recent draft of the poem, which they read nodding at the changes I had made. While not jointly written, the poem had become a shared space. By the time we were done with the drafts, the course was in its final weeks and the students had all been through the process of conceiving, arguing for and pitching a final project: a mini-manuscript, on a subject and in a style of their own choosing, that would best demonstrate what they had learned in the course. The beginner writers in the course were different already from the people to whom I had showed the first drafts, different from the people who applied for the course, different even from the people who had heard about the requirements for the final assignment a few weeks before with a mixture of dismay and joy. When I said that I was not certain that this poem was finished, they nodded a bit grimly. They were thinking of the work ahead of them. That work was the reason I had showed them the drafts and the revisions in the first place, because I was about to ask them to do the same: to ask themselves question after question as they wrote; to make hard choices; to throw out and to pull in; to mine history or images or their lives; to consider form and style and redo, redo, redo.

This is the fun part.

Not Writing

I'm not writing because everything else needs to be written.

I'm not writing because I am doing neither what I want nor what I should.

I'm not writing because some days, accomplishment is a conspiracy to make me feel better.

I'm not writing because not writing thinks it is logical, but it is subject to the same kind of perverted logic that everything else is, so I should be writing just to defy that but I'm not.

I'm not writing because of the earworm loop, six to eight bars of music that play repeatedly in my head and wrench my thoughts to one side and keep me awake, everyone says it's migraine-related except my head doesn't hurt, just six to eight bars of music writing me wrung.

I'm not writing because I read a poem in Anne Boyer's *Garments Against Women* about not writing and now I can't write about not writing without writing that and so I'm not writing because writing about not writing belongs to another not-writer.

I'm not writing because not writing is a reason to not write about not writing.

What If and Other Questions for Working Writers

> I am returning the verses with which you entrusted me. I thank
> you again for your unconditional and sincere trust. I am over-
> whelmed with it, and therefore have tried, to the best of my
> ability, to make myself a little more worthy than I, as a stranger
> to you, really am.
> – Rainer Maria Rilke, "The First Letter"

What If?

One year, in the midst of what would be my best writing year in a
long time, I was nominated for two provincial awards and one
national one. I was still a new writer and I took this, and the re-
views the books received, in stride. I took these accolades with what
I thought was professional aplomb. I did not jump up and down
and squeal, although I wanted to, and I did not tell many people.
This was aided by the fact that I was living in a new city, and did

not know many people there who I could tell. There was no social media. (Nearly unimaginable, I know, but true.) Back in my
home city, the book had been a biggish deal; not the last word in
poetry, but the owner of the bookstore where I launched sent me
a card saying that I had pulled in a record crowd. In the new city,
though, my poetry was not quite a secret and not quite a subject.
So I did what I thought was right for a peripatetic Artsy; I accepted
the nominations with what I thought was good grace, as the first
of many nominations and prizes that I would be awarded in my
brilliant career.

Are you laughing yet? This managed to be both arrogant and
naive at the same time.

When my next book came out, it was nominated for a design
award. I won a national poetry prize for one of the poems in it. It
was reviewed twice. I was having dinner at a friend's place three
months after it came out and referred to my latest book, and she
said, "What book?" I was astonished, but her question was a sharp
reminder that your own book will never be as memorable in someone else's eyes as it is in yours.

The year my third book came out I had a spectacular launch
in the city where I lived. I toured with it to four other cities. It got
no nominations and one review. It sank, like a polished and finely
designed stone, into the ocean of books published that year. It was
not a bad book, but it was just one of many.

Between that first rush of nominations and now, I have been
nominated for more awards and even won a few times, supplying
me with a short, warm glow and a few extra lines on my resume.
There is no question: it is nice to be nominated and a thrill to win,
and if you are trying to work as a full-time artist, winning a big award
can make all the difference to your readership, your sales and your
reputation. But I note that like class, admitting to not winning – or
not being nominated for prizes – is a non-starter conversation-wise.

No one knows what to say or where to look when they hear you say it. And what is there to say about not winning, or even not being nominated? This is the state in which most writers live their lives. It is not glamorous to be an unsung artist, but neither is it a purgatory of bitterness. Beginner artists do not usually hear much about the book that does well but not spectacularly, though it is very common. Writers with serious chops publish all the time with a splash, and then they sell fairly well until they don't. The gold star of writing a classic that is reprinted multiple times and beloved by readers everywhere – or argued over by readers everywhere, which is also a gold-star strategy – happens, of course, but that's like Hollywood or winning the lottery. I worry when I meet young artists that they have unrealistic standards for themselves: bestseller by twenty-five or movie deal by thirty. The reason not everyone does it is because there is no formula for doing it. If you know how to write a bestseller, go for it. But if you don't know how to write a bestseller yet, you need to practice. If you are writing solely for the purposes of acknowledgement, this can seem bleak. How do we keep going without the boost provided by the trappings of outward success?

Community is one answer, because within it, you can learn to make space for your work and the work of others. Poet Rob Winger notes that our cravings for community sometimes spring fully formed into our young heads:

I distinctly remember, in high school, having this idea: that perhaps, somewhere, I could found – or find – some sort of society of people who discussed conceptual ideas about what it all meant, and why. I was too blind or dumb or raw to realize that philosophy, religious tradition and academic discourses already existed; but, in retrospect, my stumbling, awkward conceptualization of what was essentially all communal, intellectual engagement in ideas perhaps epitomizes what I felt was the absolute absence of artistic discourse in my upbringing, at least in the manner that it's popularly conceived.

Rob's description of these first thoughts of what an enlivening practice might look like is – for all his modesty – pretty clear in its interest in finding a way to meet with others and honour your own practice. It's a lifelong project. Think of yourself as someone building a house, and the accomplishment of finishing it piece by piece. Think, too, that like building a house, forging an artistic practice means that sometimes you are going to have to stop and talk to others who are doing the same thing: for direction, for solidarity, for ideas. This is especially vital as you begin the first draft of your practice. As Leena Niemela notes: "I didn't know that a 'writer's practice' was a thing until I had a writer's community who talked about how they structured their time, how they generated new work on a regular basis and how they revised pieces over time." It's more definitely a thing in a community, and so are the sometimes queasy, heady moments when you first start to name your practice, out loud, to yourself and others. Leena again: "I needed to know that the act of writing was enough; that I didn't need to publish, or read publicly to consider myself a writer." It's important to learn how to name your art for yourself and how to talk about art, yours and that of others. When you learn this in a class or workshop – anything with a designated leader – this might not seem so urgent. You may find yourself thinking, "I don't really have to be good at discussing work or making thoughtful comments – the leader will do that." This is certainly true, but every course and workshop is time-limited. Your turn to lead is coming soon – maybe a lot sooner than you think. Learn to praise books and other art in a meaningful way: with attention and content and questions. I always think of the writer who told me that a writer's most valuable skill is generosity: to read someone else's book and recommend it genuinely to others.

Artists have to be good at deferring gratification. As a poet, I practice short written forms and can draft a poem in a day, polish it over a few months and send it out to a journal. If the journal is the kind that is always on top of things and practices a fast turn-around time for submissions, the poem might be published within a month, but it is much more usual to have a six- to eight-month reading period before you hear back and then if they accept it, another two- to four-month lag before it shows up in print. No one is dragging their feet or trying to torture you with their slowness; that's just the pace of literary magazine publishing. Of course, most of those editors are artists with day jobs, too. If that seems like a long time to you, remember that it is lightning fast compared to writing a short story or an essay, and the blink of an eye for a novelist. Artists learn to be happy with a day's work because most days that is all we have. It is a good way to live in the twenty-first century when so few people see the material evidence of their work. It's even harder to see evidence of accomplishment in your working day if you are working in any customer-service-oriented profession where you see people only if something goes wrong, and never when things are operating smoothly. What then can you show as your work, as what you "made" today? Art is very good for this, if you know how to see progress in your own work. This is a valuable skill to develop. Craftspeople have known this for centuries.

Winnipeg writer Ariel Gordon mused about money when I asked, and noted that artists have to think a lot about priorities and sometimes about stepping out of line with a capitalist existence of constant acquisition: "I've chosen to focus on my writing and it almost never pays. It feels like we can't afford our life. But I mostly love the life we've built and how supportive my partner is; I know I'm lucky to have been able to choose. So: Do what makes you happy. Work hard. Invest in community. Ask to be paid for your work but don't focus overmuch on money. Think hard on what you need to live; is a house/car possible or even needed?" Choosing what to have in your life is a constant process, and I don't think that Ariel is advocating for a romantic (or real) poverty here, but rather something quite practical: a series of considered choices that make your practice possible. Learn what you need, and more importantly, what you don't.

Let's say that you do all the good things. You write, you read, you perform, you consult and create community, you are generous and diverse and eclectic in your tastes, you enjoy everyone else's art when you get a chance to take it in, and still, despite your efforts, you make most of your money doing something else. You are not a household name. You never win a big award. You write some books and you even have readers, but most days – and indeed most years because books take time – it is just you and your drafts. Let's say that at the end of the average month, your time is 20 per cent spent on making your art, 40 per cent spent on being a good parent or partner or sibling or offspring or friend or person in the world, and 40 per cent spent on doing a job that keeps the wolf from the door, and you and your loved ones in groceries and a roof over your head. (Let's also say that you even like that job, some of the time.) Let's say you never become famous, except in a small way in your community.

Is that depressing? I don't mean for it to be. It is the unvarnished truth about the lives of most artists. We do it because we love it. We do it because it makes sense of the world for us. In the hyper-Warholian present/future, when everyone is famous for fifteen seconds, accountability is precarious and ceaseless self-promotion is the currency on social media, what is fame? What is success?

How Do I?

I saw a very fine amateur performance of a favourite musical a little while ago; it was a production in which I didn't know anyone. My friends and I went because we were in another city and able to indulge whims in ways we couldn't always when at home.

First, a word about community theatre: always go when you have the chance. Don't hesitate. Part of what makes amateur theatre so electric is that you get to see people doing what they have willingly given up time and money to do, and what they might (occasionally) lack in skill, they will more than make up for in delight at being onstage. These are artists who know what it is all about: doing it, trying it, taking risks. I guarantee that you will see people having a whale of a time, transported by the chance to make art. I am not the only one who thinks so.

So, picture it: we're in the audience, my travelling pals and me, and people are singing like they invented song, and the production has a fun new angle that I haven't seen explored before – and even with that one performer who upstages everyone like her life depends upon it, the cast is really strong and the voices are awesome and it's the best twenty dollars I've spent in ages. One performer, though, rises to the top of the heap. He is, as they used to say when I was a performer, "the Whole Package." If he's onstage, we're not looking anywhere else; even the Dedicated Upstager can't pull our attention away from him. He blows our minds in the final production number, and when it ends we stand for the ovation and then flop down in our seats and exclaim, "*that* was fantastic!" Then we are swept outside with the crowd, where the performers are in a reception line like at a wedding. We line up with everyone else, friends and neighbours and local business owners, and when I reach the Whole Package, I tell him how awesome his performance was. I see him blink a little at my compliment, and then he thanks me and the moment is over and we are back in the car.

A few weeks later, I was wondering what it was about that performance that made it so great. Who *was* that guy? I checked the program and googled the performer. He wasn't hard to find. I found the website of his home renovation business – a family business that employed three generations. This did not fit my picture of his work, but then I read the testimonials. I saw that in that business, where people are almost always tense and vulnerable, worried about money, worried about their homes and about making a mistake, people who had employed his company said exactly the kinds of things that I had been thinking about his performance in the musical. People wrote about his passion, his presentness, his style, his support, his integrity. I know that a PR person could have fabricated those testimonials, but I was struck by how clearly the comments aligned with my experience of this performer. It was as though all these people had seen his performance in the musical, when he was so clearly and manifestly present. Making art gives us all a chance to bring our best selves to everything we do.

I think of the physician poet Dannie Abse, and the care and attention of his work in medicine surfacing in poems like "Between 3 and 4 a.m." or "X Ray." Or Cathy Park Hong's work poems in *Engine Empire*, which refuse to discuss work as fulfilling but instead shift its mundane moments into surreality. Kurt Vonnegut Jr. has written extensively about his years working in public relations for General Electric, where his day job was to communicate esoteric scientific ideas to the general public. The task of doing so, day in, day out, gave him ideas for the short stories he was writing at night, and for the premise for two of his bestselling novels: *Player Piano*, some of which he set in GE's Schenectady plant, and *Cat's Cradle*, based on Nobel Prize–winner Dr. Irving Langmuir's work with artificial rainfall. There is far too much talk about how art is rarefied and exists in isolation when exactly the opposite is true: writers get ideas from reading everything, from grocery lists to George Saunders, from tweets to Jane Jacobs, from Plato to Eileen Myles. They also get them from working a day job.

More than one excellent artist has found themselves at thirty, at thirty-five, at forty, wondering why, despite doing everything right, despite their talent and their hard work and their ambition, they haven't "made it" yet. Think carefully about what "making it" means. Success and failure are extremely relative. I often worry that the only artistic role models available to beginners are people making tons of money and getting adoring crowds. That's not the fault of the beginner artists; we can only see what we are told to consume unless we are offered other examples. For every bestseller, there are thousands of writers who are successful in that they write often and well, and have books that are published and read. Many excellent writers don't make it to bestseller lists and they keep doing it anyway. Artists need to be sensitive, but they also need to be tough.

Writers do not speak enough about the loneliness of our profession, and it is hard to say whether writers are lonely because they are writers or if they become writers because they understand aloneness. I will not solve that conundrum, but I do not want to pretend that isolation is not a real concern for out-of-line artists. It most definitely is. I write about community and working with mentors, which assumes that you will have or can create such opportunities, but the truth is that they are not always there and sometimes your ability to create change may be limited. Sometimes you have colleagues but they are busy. Sometimes you will have no local colleagues. What then?

I was not kidding about valuing and developing the strength that comes from cultivating a rich inner life, because sometimes it will have to sustain you over long periods of time. Like the years until your kids are all in school, or the years it takes you to get more established in your day job and have time for your art, or for the months when you put everything on hold to care for the sick or injured or elderly. Life can be very rough on art, and it will be hard to maintain a practice, without interruption, throughout such life events. When I was caring for my mother in the last weeks of her life, I did not go home at night and write elegies. I was exhausted; I went home and slept, got up in the morning and went to the hospital. That was it. I also didn't go home after her funeral and begin to record my experience. It was months later that I started to write something about the experience, and years before the elegies themselves started getting published. Sometimes you will need to draw on your strength to make something necessary. A former student of mine, Cree writer Corri Arnold-Daniels, has said that writing about being a Sixties Scoop survivor was a way to come to her grief and find herself in the process. That didn't happen all at once: "I had an essay exam in 1984 while I was in grade ten. We had just read *The Wars* by Timothy Findley. My teacher, Mr. Merkel, drew these huge checkmarks in red marker all over the page and I received an A on the paper. He then asked me to write a story. Which I did. Thirty-three years later, I wrote 'Sweetgrass Spirits,' a short story I wrote to help me heal from the news of the death of my brother, and it was longlisted on the CBC Short Story Prize in 2017. In both instances, I felt the same happiness. I am a writer." Corri's identification of that "same happiness" sustained over thirty-three years is notable not only for its resiliency but also for the way that writing one story gave her courage to write another, and then a harder story still. Artists aren't factories; we may make objects from our experience, but like anything worth doing, that takes time and it means believing people – like Mr. Merkel – who believe in us. As poet Micheline Maylor puts it, "My relationship with fear has been one where fear returns like a recurring nightmare and the only thing to do is to slay the daemon and be the superhero of my own life."

When the sun is shining, make hay. When you have the chance to study, to read, to argue, to workshop, to practice, do it. Lean times are always just a breath away for any artist. Take every chance you have to root your practice, your habits, your knowledge and understanding, not only so you can have it at your fingertips but also because you are going to have to leave it sometimes. Build it solidly enough in your consciousness that when you return after an absence, of weeks or months or, yes, years, you will be able to walk back into the house you have built and remind yourself where everything is. Your practice is always yours. The beauty of artmaking is that no one can take it away from you. You did it; you made it. If they burn it, you can make another. If they ignore it, you can make thousands of them uninterrupted. If you look at it and think it's not very good, you can make a better one – or a million better ones. But you need to find a way to keep going, to keep improving, to do the work whether or not people are cheering for you. You will feel lonely, often with good reason. Social media can be excellent for staying connected, but sometimes it makes me feel like the loneliest person on the planet. The loneliness is the bad news. The slightly better news is that everyone feels lonely anyway, so at least you get to do it with an artistic practice in your pocket.

A life of literary citizenship is hard for many people to imagine. During a busy week, even after twenty-five years of publishing what I write, I sometimes suffer that failure of the imagination, as well. Much work that happens to assist and create the literary world, especially in smaller places, is nearly invisible, but in reading, writing, teaching, reviewing and otherwise promoting work, we make the community. Striving-class artists are often geniuses at flying beneath the radar, which is why you need to look for us carefully; we know how to hide in plain sight. Maybe the best part of knowing that you are out of line is the permission it gives you to step further out of line, and to learn how to appear before anyone can see you approach.

Poet Laurie D. Graham, author of *Settler Education*, notes that figuring out how to maintain a balance between writing time and earning opportunities is both the pulse of the creative life and its biggest puzzle:

> Wage-earning remains the biggest obstacle. I need an amount of what Karen Mulhallen once called "psychic space" in order to write, and I've had to balance this need with the need to stay housed. At numerous points, work has taken up all my brain space and sometimes all my time. I do a lot more crying when this happens. I'm a lot more brittle and rage-filled. I can recognize this in myself now, and I'm better at keeping the wage-earning to its own roughly finite compartment. And I'm a bit less precious about my writing time and will take it when I can get it rather than wait for perfect environmental conditions to roll in. But getting into the habit of protecting one's time is one that I had to learn and am still working on. I'm always concocting ways to buy or make that "psychic space" for myself.

That psychic space is all-important to your practice. Laurie's notion that it takes constant negotiation to establish it and maintain it is a point well taken. The pulse of that creative life is not separate from your life but a vital part of the whole.

But here is a hypothetical situation: say that six months after you take that influential course or meet that new group of artists, you find yourself in a more isolated position. Maybe you've moved or taken a different job or your life responsibilities have changed and you can no longer connect often with your artistic community. Take a deep breath – take several – and treat your practice as though it is worthy of your time and attention. Nurture your artistic impulses like they matter, even if all you are doing is acknowledging them in your head. Be your own teacher. Challenge yourself to do it better and do it differently. Isolation from other artists is hard. It is one reason why people move to a big city, but that's not possible all the time for everyone.

And even when it is physically possible, it is often financially unlikely, as young artists in Toronto or Vancouver have told me for years. How they live in order to afford rent and food in those cities stretches them thin, sometimes too thin to practice the art that they came to the city to develop. It no longer surprises me to read of more people who are choosing to live in smaller cities where they can afford to feed themselves even if it means isolation from the hustle and sophistication of a big city. There are whole bunches of us out here in the (relative) hinterlands, writing: Sonnet L'Abbé in Nanaimo, Gregory Scofield in Sudbury, Roxane Gay in Indiana. I think too of the fiction writer Shirley Jackson, living in the classist, sometimes anti-Semitic community of North Bennington, Vermont, which now celebrates her work with an annual Shirley Jackson Day. This town was at least partially responsible for giving the hair-raising violence of her fiction its class-conscious edge, and Shirley Jackson Day is celebrated each June 26, one day before the day of "The Lottery" in her short story of the same name.

But What If No One?

What you've always suspected is true. No one understands you.

I know that no one understands me. This is actually a relief to admit against the background of the relentless cheeriness of online culture. It can be dispiriting to spend your artistic life shuttling between extreme joy and profound despair. Harder to forge, but much more useful, is the median position: one in which you see yourself as neither the Original Genius nor a Lowly Worm, but a Working Writer. The Original Genius and a Lowly Worm will seem infinitely available to you in your early years of making art, and some days you will move through three of four iterations of them a day. But the extremes are not your friends. Adrenaline does not last: that heady rush, that world-beating, problem-solving, perfect-phrase feeling. Artists need to store that feeling like a bear stores fat for the winter, for the moment when you return to the desk and to your revisions.

When you first begin, try a thousand different things: different forms, different voices, different tones, personae, languages, ways of writing, exercises, stimuli, constraints. Discomfort shakes you up, makes you see things differently and sometimes gets you to argue for or against something you believed was a given.

When you first begin, take in everything you can. Be willing to be surprised, moved, offended, enlightened and sceptical. Be willing to say, *that's good but I could do that, or better*, and then do it.

When you first begin, consider this, from fiction writer Lauren B. Davis: "Keep the drama out of your life so you can get it on the page instead."

When you first begin, try staying accountable to some kind of external influence: a group, a class, even a friend with the same interests. Meet often, even when you don't feel like it. Enter into a social contract to produce work quickly and to a set of standards. Don't worry about a grand plan. Produce work. Make stuff. Many of us desire experimentation, but we often fear it. *Will this change my process?* beginners ask me. The answer is, *yes, it will, if you're fortunate*.

My lifelong goal as an artist is to become more and more myself while making stranger and stranger things, things that take me out of myself. I hear an awful lot of my own voice, internally or speaking aloud, and reading (and writing) to hear someone else's voice relaxes part of my brain that is perpetually revved during the average weekday. If I had to say what the therapeutic benefit of writing is for me personally, I would name the ability to focus into a relaxed mind. Don't worry if you aren't doing that, or even if it doesn't make sense to you. That's what making art does for me: it will inevitably do something different for you.

Who's in My Corner?

I read acknowledgements at the ends of books with fervour, because I always want to know how authors sustain themselves throughout the making of a book. Sometimes funding bodies are thanked, or residencies that gave the author space and time to work. That is useful information, but I want to see who supplied the unglamorous workaday material and emotional assistance: who had faith, who made the coffee and watched the kids, who read the first drafts and said, "I like this." Those are important people. Authors also thank people who didn't do (or didn't seem to do) much, but may have said the thing that sparked a turning point in the book.

A practice takes dedication. Dedication is slow and it does not come from nowhere. Its biggest challenge will be that you have to learn it and observe it, and consider it valuable even when others do not. And there will always be others who do not.

Am I Doing It?

Sing in the shower. Dance to the radio. Tell stories. Write a poem to a friend, even a lousy poem. Do it as well as you possibly can. You will get an enormous reward. You will have created something.
– Kurt Vonnegut Jr., *A Man Without a Country*

I love writing. It is my happy place. I love having nothing else to do but write, even if it only lasts for twenty minutes. I have a very crowded head, and writing quiets the noise for me: not always and not always completely, but enough and more than anything else I've tried. This wasn't always the case. I can remember when I first started trying to do something with poetry: I would have been about twenty and not especially good at writing, but I was as intense as all get-out. In those years, writing did not quiet my crowded noisy head; it was more like having to listen to a shouting stream of voices, yanking the words out of it like salmon from a stream. They were slippery; it was exhausting. The poems were often derivative. But this odd method pleased me – and only me. I did it enough that dragging the words out of the smoking river of my consciousness became a kind of pleasure and I stopped worrying about what it all meant. I had the great advantage at that point of my life to no longer be at any stage of formal education. And while it was hard figuring out my waking life, I could feel my writing self gaining strength, and soon enough I dared to sit in a room with strangers and call myself a writer. I knew what it was like to be young and audacious and let the chips fall where they may. Practice and reading and kind suggestions from a host of other writers wrought something else: a way to quiet the roar so that I did not need to fish from the word stream. And I could listen to my voice in my own head.

No one will stop you from quitting artmaking. Maybe you will be lucky and have a partner who won't let you quit, or a publisher who keeps asking for a manuscript, but mostly, artists have to be self-starters, self-producers, in love with the process, willing to explore without being praised, happy to create without being encouraged. Deepen your practice. Your life will thank you.

Coda: Reading the Dead Girl's Books

When I was thirteen, the young adult daughter of my parents' friends' died; she committed suicide. I was never told why. It's possible that neither my parents nor hers knew why. She was twenty and so much older than me; she lived in a different world, the way it is at that age, when seven years might as well be seven light years. I didn't know her, though I may have met her when I was too young to remember. I heard about her death long after it happened, when her parents were at our house for dinner, and I could tell from the odd lull in the adults' conversation that something was not right. I could see that Mrs. K_____ was tearing up, and because I grew up in a buckled-down era with a stoic family, I had never seen an adult cry – certainly not Mrs. K_____ who I had known all my life as a woman neither conciliatory nor sunny, but wry and sharp-tongued, unafraid of disagreement when talk turned to politics at those dinners, as it always did. The sight of her face hitching and eyes reddening at our dinner table was so alarming that when I asked about it later, my mother couldn't dissemble. She said H_____, the

K_____s' daughter, had died by suicide. I don't remember what I thought. I didn't get very far when I tried to think of why someone might kill themselves. I didn't know enough about her, or about anything.

Sometime later I inherited H_____'s poetry books – Leonard Cohen's *Selected Poems* and *Flowers for Hitler* – and it seemed then that the mystery might be solvable. My mother stood at my bedroom door with the books, offering them to me like the strange gifts they were. To be clear, it wasn't unusual for me to get second-hand items from the daughters of my parents' friends. My girl cousins all lived far away, and so while my in-town boy cousins conducted a brisk trade between themselves in used toys, my sources always came from farther afield.

I still have these books. They are in my office, with the other girl's name written on the fly-leaves, some poems marked with a large X beside them ("The Failure of a Secular Life," "Leviathan" and "Heirloom") in *Flowers for Hitler*, which also bears a stamp on page thirty-three from a Winnipeg high school library. The first page, where the pocket for the lending card would have been glued, has been torn out, and the tape that fastened the call number to the spine still sticks to the front cover. Both books were dog-eared and knocked about when I inherited them; they were demonstrably much-read, important to the young woman who owned them. The ex-library-book status of this copy of *Flowers for Hitler* – a fifth imprint released in 1968 – suggests that she may have stolen the book from the school library because she liked it so much, and that she was inspired by this first book to purchase her copy of Cohen's *Selected Poems* (a fourth printing from March 1969) a year or two later. The publisher's release of these reprints of the two books so close together speaks to Cohen's immense popularity at the time, in those post-Centennial Pierre Trudeau–era years. McClelland and

Stewart clearly knew a hot commodity when they saw one, and they published Cohen accordingly.

What does it mean to inherit a dead girl's books? In M. Scott Peck's *People of the Lie*, the American psychiatrist retells an infamous story of a couple who, after their elder son committed suicide by shotgun, "gifted" their younger surviving son with the older boy's weapon. According to Peck, the message is implicit and horrible: you're next, go now and do likewise. Peck reports that the parents protested that they were not well off and that the shotgun was an expensive item, that they did not wish to say anything with the gift but rather logically redistribute the dead boy's worldly goods to someone who could use the gun for hunting, citing the younger boy's now-inherited responsibilities to help to furnish food for the rural family. When I first heard this, I was aghast, especially since the friend with whom I was discussing it had an older brother who had died by suicide. The cruelty of those parents seemed to be in the room with us as we talked. But I wonder about it now, not that I especially wish to absolve anyone, or could even if I wanted to. Peck was speaking of a context outside of his social class, and he was swift and sure in his judgement as only a certain kind of medical professional can be.

Now, decades later, I know too well that when people die, their stuff doesn't dissolve into thin air. It has to go somewhere: to the attic or basement, to friends, to charity, to the dump. I know that imprudent decisions are made all the time by mourning families who are grieving and sleep-deprived and occupy a completely different world from people who can still see all of their loved ones in one room. I think of Cohen's moody books, full of poems of despair and lust and suicide and torture and Holocaust-survivor guilt, and now that I am older than my mother was when she stood in the doorway with the books in her hands, I admit that it is odd to give another child a dead girl's books that were so scored by violence, both personal and historical.

But we were a starving-class family undergoing a shift into being striving-class. I lived in a world where "waste not, want not" was an unbreakable law. I understood that we didn't have money the way some of my friends' families did, and to refuse "perfectly good" items when they were offered to me was not really an option. This was known as "turning up your nose" and it was a very particular Protestant sin. It meant that you thought you were too good for things; at best you were a snob, and at worst you were deluded. If I didn't like a thing that was offered to me, I knew there would be dozens of chances to pass it on to someone else later. Except if a family member gave it to me as a birthday gift and then there was no getting rid of it. Ever.

It would be easy to draw a line from Cohen's poems, chronicling his own well-known struggles with depression and the frequent appearance of the word *suicide* in his early work, and claim that reading these books contributed to the young woman's death. But I don't think people live – or die – like that. Looking at the poems she marked, the books seem helpful to her mental state rather than hurtful, as though they provided solace when little else could until, finally, nothing helped. This very well may be a case of me projecting my reading experience on to the books, or me resisting the reading that books are murderous.

As my mother stood in the doorway, I could see that the books were clear evidence of a sophisticated world; the covers showed Cohen's profile gazing off to the right, wistful, handsome. The books had belonged to an older girl, after all, and they pretty much screamed contraband: books that I would not have been allowed to read if my parents had read them first. My best friend had a copy of the underground classic *Go Ask Alice*, which had plenty of drug use and sexual freedom, and we knew that such books were designed to be hidden from parents. But here my mother was handing these books over like she was the most permissive parent in the world. When I opened *Flowers for Hitler*, I could see the first poem had the word *nymphomaniac* in it. Chalk one up for the intimidation factor of poetry because I don't think my parents even cracked the covers.

It was obvious the books were cool: Montreal cool, big city cool, sexy cool. They were also my first indication that poetry could be political. Poems were titled "All There is to Know About Adolph Eichmann" and "Goebbels Abandons His Novel and Joins the Party," and there were lines like "is there anything emptier / than the drawer where / you used to store your opium?" There were poems in which Cohen tossed around words like *torture* and *cuckold*, and *Flowers for Hitler* contains a play script, "The New Step: A Ballet-Drama in One Act," which openly defies standards of beauty and ends with a fat girl dancing in her apartment and telling her thin roommate that she'll dance any way she wants. I had no idea what to think, and I would no more ask someone about it than I would cut off my own arm. And whom could I ask? My friends? My teachers? My minister? I just read and reread and reread again. It was, in some ways, an excellent introduction to the basic tasks of literary analysis. I spent a long time puzzling over a book that was both accessible and baffling: one that I could read, but that I couldn't quite understand.

And who was my benefactor, the girl who bought and stole these books, who wrote in them and marked her favourites? It was a *Great Expectations* moment, with H_____ as my Magwitch, transported to another world. But Magwitch does return, transformed and seeking social revenge, and H_____ has not. My parents are both dead and so are hers, and there's no one left to ask about her or about her love of Leonard Cohen's work. I can only make of her what I can from the books themselves, in literary forensic fashion, as markers on a map of someone's life. So many years later, I am looking not for why she killed herself because I don't think that is contained in those books. I am looking for how she lived and what she loved, and I know that as I do so, every answer I get will be at best a trace, absence scratched onto absence. For instance, when I read H_____'s books as an adult, I wonder what the S written beside some poems in the table of contents stands for. I checked *suicide* first, partly because Cohen mentions it several times in the poems, and partly because, however salacious or unfair, I was working with one of the few concrete pieces of information I had about H_____. But suicide didn't turn up in any of the poems marked with an S. Other words didn't quite fit: *Sex? Scars? Sleep? Songs?* "Suzanne Takes You Down," arguably Cohen's best-known poem and song, is not marked with an S but instead with a tiny slanted pencil mark beside it in the table of contents: neither a checkmark nor a comma. "Pagans" and "Story," both from *Let Us Compare Mythologies*, also have that small slanted mark found in the *Selected*'s table of contents. "The Music Crept By Us" and "What I'm Doing Here" are dog-eared; other poems' page numbers are circled in the index of first lines. If it was a code, I could not crack it.

I returned to the largest marks in *Flowers for Hitler*, three big bold Xs marked beside the poems in the body of the text. All three poems were about torture and pain and the unbearable atmosphere of modern industrial capitalism that offers no solace. It is up to the poem itself to see and to say what it sees, repeating whenever the reader returned to the pages. The context, for all three poems, suggests Cohen's consideration of Theodor Adorno's admonition in his 1949 essay "Cultural Criticism and Society" that "to write poetry after Auschwitz is barbaric," and that if "cultural intelligence" is to survive, it must move away from what Adorno calls "self-satisfied contemplation." Later, in 1966's *Negative Dialectics*, Adorno retracted part of this statement to say that "perennial suffering has as much right to expression as a tortured man has to scream," but also that those who survived, "by way of atonement he will be plagued by dreams such as that he is no longer living at all." This may seem like heady stuff for a young Jewish man from Montreal to be writing about, and even more unusual for two young Christian women from the Prairies to be thinking about. Then and now, I can only speak for myself. While there was much in Cohen's poems that I did not understand when I first read them, I could discern the shape of the pain in Cohen's "Heirloom": "The torture scene developed under a glass bell / such as might protect an expensive clock." The poem saw me; my relief was in finding this language that spoke about cruelty as I had been introduced to it. Cruelty and its social preservation were already embedded in my life. This is sometimes how we learn to read: through empathy, through finding out that someone else's pain and the history that accompanies it illuminates the unnameable in our own minds. Equivalence is not usual, nor is it necessary for good writing and passionate reading; I still don't know how Cohen made our realities overlap for several lines at a time. And I don't know what H_____ was thinking when she read this; she marked these poems for reasons of her own. As advances, even provisional ones, are made in the diagnosis and treatment of depression, I've thought of her often, and how much what might then have been beyond medical intervention or assistance would have been treatable only a decade later. Or not. This too is just a guess, and most days it seems wrong to think that I know her or could presume to understand her reasons.

Whenever you read a used book that has been lovingly marked by its previous owner, you're reading two texts simultaneously: the version printed on the page, and the other, hovering slightly above it, marked and circled by the previous owner. At thirteen, I needed all the help I could get. I absorbed Cohen's words and H_____'s reading practices. When I posted a photo of these two books on my Facebook page in 2017 as part of a series I was curating on vintage

Canadian poetry books, the books received a deluge of testimonies from writer friends, all of whom chimed in that these were the first poetry books they ever bought, owned or smuggled home from the library. I don't know their reasons, either.

When I studied Cohen's poems in university, one of my professors called him "creepy," and I had to admit that this is sometimes true and is even noted on the back cover of *Selected* in an unattributed blurb that calls Cohen "a beautiful creep." Such early influences can have long-term effects, especially when they are accidental. Like families, we can't choose our influences, simply because we don't yet know how. Sometimes, they come walking in your door, borne on the back of grief and happenstance and guilt. The two Cohen books on my shelf travelled from H_____'s apartment in Toronto, packed up and brought to Winnipeg by her devastated parents who didn't know what they should do or could do with their beloved daughter's prized possessions. I don't know why or how they thought of me for the books, but my guess is that they didn't want to throw them away, yet they couldn't bear to have them in their house. Somehow, my mother agreed to take the books and give them to her voracious reader kid, perhaps because she too did not know the right thing to do. That uncertainty is mine now. The four adults, the K_____s and my parents, would be friends for the rest of their lives. Time passed and I grew older than H_____ was when she died. I moved to Toronto as she had. I took the Cohen books with me and lived through university degrees and boring jobs and bad boyfriends and an aggressive tumour that landed me in hospital and recovery and a few more cities.

The Cohen books sit on the shelf in my office, their scuffed covers at odds with the gleaming spines and saturated colours of newer poetry books. I don't open them often. Life is long and it is shockingly short. Sometimes pieces of someone else's history come flying at you out of a dark cumulus you can't see through. You can't know what you'll inherit, or from who, and you don't have to make sense of it. Those books weren't meant for me, but I reached up and caught them from the cloud and then they were mine to puzzle out or ignore as I chose. Part influence and part action, part obsession and part negative capability: my out-of-line place.

Acknowledgements

No book is written in isolation, and even the most emboldened artists don't make themselves from whole cloth. I thank my late parents, Jack and Norma MacDonald, for protecting my reading time. My early mentors were many: Tom Chan at River Heights Junior High, and Muriel Jamieson and Jim Bulloch at Kelvin High School in Winnipeg; Susan Ioannou, Helen Humphreys, Robert Priest and Betsy Struthers for their instruction in poetry; Neil Besner, Catherine Hunter and Dennis Cooley for intellectual and creative community in Winnipeg. In Toronto, Ian Kennedy and Tamara Elliott were the best peer mentors.

Without my savvy out-of-line students over the past five years I wouldn't have written any of this down. Their steady gaze and good questions keep me thinking. Many people shared their experiences of arts communities and class: thanks to Lillian Allen, Jacob McArthur Mooney, Pearl Pirie, Jane Eaton Hamilton, Laurie D. Graham, Dorothy Palmer, Meharoona Ghani, Joanna Lilley, derek beaulieu, Kim Clark, Janice Lee, Canisia Lubrin, Ariel Gordon, Brenda Schmidt, Yvonne Blomer, Kit Dobson, Maureen Hynes, Micheline Maylor, Corri Arnold-Daniels, Ashley Hommel-Hynd, Kyleen McGragh, Liz Ukrainetz, Leena Niemela, Lauren B. Davis,

Sylvia Symons, a. charlie peters and Rob Winger for contributing their comments. And to Chris Banks for recommending Hugo's *The Triggering Town*.

The Electronic Garretians are the best online writing group an out-of-line writer could ask for. Thanks to Tanja Saari Bartel, Maureen Hynes, Maureen Scott Harris, Leena Niemela, Brenda Schmidt, Ariel Gordon, Cary O'Malley, Shannon Maguire, Micheline Maylor, Jane Eaton Hamilton, Bren Simmers, Miranda Pearson and Yvonne Blomer for being there for all the hard questions. Frances Sprout was my first and most encouraging reader of these chapters in their nascent states. Jenny Kerber and Veronica Austen always made it seem like sitting down to write together was the most exciting use of our time. My colleagues at the Department of English and Film Studies at Wilfrid Laurier University not only allow but also understand my dual identity, a comprehension that is hard to come by and for which I know I do not thank them enough. Special shout-out to my colleagues who teach fiction writing, Tamas Dobozy and Mariam Pirbhai.

Noelle Allen's team at Wolsak and Wynn get everything done with style and good humour; thanks to Ashley Hisson for her on-the-ball savvy and Andrew Wilmot for his keen eye on the text. Noelle was the first to say she thought there was a book in this, and her belief brought it into focus for me.

John Roscoe has nurtured my eccentricities for more than two decades. Baby, you're the greatest.

Notes

"This is for You" was inspired by blog posts on seeing and acknowledging peer reviewers and contract faculty written by Lily Cho and Erin Wunker, respectively, both published in 2015 on the website *Hook & Eye: Fast Feminism, Slow Academe.* Thanks to the artists with whom I shared a stage during the Mysterious Barricades performance of September 2017, especially the musicianship of Kathryn Ladano with whom I performed "This is for You."

Portions of "The Writer Next Door: A Finding Place" appeared as "Who Do You Think? Reading Sarah Klassen through Alice Munro" in *11 Encounters with Mennonite Fiction* (Mennonite Literary Society, 2017). Thanks to Hildi Froese Tiessen for giving me the chance to think back through Munro.

A shorter version of "How to Stage a Process Installation" won the Robert Kroetsch Teaching Award with the Canadian Creative Writers and Writing Programs in 2017. My thanks to the judges, with special gratitude to my students of EN370: Creative Writing: Poetry in Fall 2016 at Wilfrid Laurier University for their curiosity and generosity in that exercise. Parts of this book grew from occasions when I was invited to speak, and I thank Aritha van Herk and Christl Verduyn for the chance to try out material from chapter two as "Working, Class, Woman" at the Speaking Her Mind conference at the University of Calgary in October 2016. Thanks also to Colleen Winter for her invitation to speak to the Orillia Writers Group in June 2017 at the Stephen Leacock House.

I saw Joan Hotchkis perform her one-woman show *Tearsheets: Letters I Didn't Send Home* at the Edinburgh Festival in 1992; it lingered. Brava.

Works Cited

Adorno, Theodor. "Cultural Criticism and Society." 1949. Trans. Samuel and Shierry Weber. *Prisms*. MIT Press, 1983.

——. *Negative Dialectics*. Trans. E.B. Ashton. Routledge, 1966.

Barry, Lynda *One! Hundred! Demons!* Montreal: Drawn & Quarterly, 2005.

Boyer, Anne. *Garments Against Women*. Boise: Ahsahta Press, 2015.

Brand, Dionne. *Inventory*. Toronto: McClelland & Stewart, 2006.

Brandt, Di. *Dancing Naked: Narrative Strategies for Writing Across Centuries*. Toronto: Mercury Press, 1996.

Cohen, Leonard. *Flowers for Hitler*. Toronto: McClelland & Stewart, 1964.

——. *Selected Poems, 1956-1968*. Toronto: McClelland & Stewart, 1968.

Compton, Wayde. *49th Parallel Psalm*. Vancouver: Arsenal Pulp Press, 1999.

Dzodan, Flavia. "My Feminism Will Be Intersectional or it Will Be Bullshit!" *Tiger Beatdown*. 10 October 2011.

Fiske, Susan T. *Envy Up, Scorn Down: How Status Divides Us*. New York: Russell Sage, 2011.

Fussell, Paul. *Class: A Guide Through the American Status System*. New York: Summit, 1983.

Gibson, Margaret. *The Butterfly Ward*. Ottawa: Oberon Press, 1976.

Goldberg, Natalie. *Writing Down the Bones: Freeing the Writer Within*. Boulder: Shambhala, 1986.

hooks, bell. *Where We Stand: Class Matters*. New York: Routledge, 2000.

Hugo, Richard. *The Triggering Town*. 1979. New York: WW Norton, 2010.

Kellner, Thomas. "Kurt's Cradle." *GE Reports*. 30 November 2016.

Kübler-Ross, Elisabeth. *On Death and Dying*. New York: Simon & Schuster, 1969.

Leguizamo, John, and Christo Cassano. *Ghetto Klown*. New York: Abrams ComicArts, 2015.

Long Soldier, Layli. *WHEREAS: poems*. Minneapolis: Graywolf Press, 2017.

Lorde, Audre. *Sister Outsider*. Freedom, CA: Crossing Press, 1984.

Michaels, Anne. *The Weight of Oranges*. Toronto: Coach House, 1985.

Morris, Toby. "The Pencilsword: On a Plate." *The Wireless*. 22 May 2015.

Munro, Alice. *Dance of the Happy Shades*. Toronto: Ryerson Press, 1968.

Munro, Sheila. *Lives of Mothers and Daughters: Growing Up with Alice Munro*. Toronto: McClelland & Stewart, 2002.

Olds, Sharon. Interview with Kaveh Akbar. *Divedapper* 38. 28 December 2015.

Peck, M. Scott. *People of the Lie: The Hope for Healing Human Evil*. New York: Simon & Schuster, 1983.

Pratt, Minnie Bruce. "Identity: Skin Blood Heart." *Yours in Struggle: Three Feminist Perspectives on Anti-Semitism and Racism*. Ithaca, NY: Firebrand, 1984.

Queyras, Sina. Interview with Heather Milne. *Prismatic Publics: Innovative Canadian Women's Poetry and Poetics*. Eds. Kate Eichhorn and Heather Milne. Toronto: Coach House Press, 2009.

Rankine, Claudia. *Citizen: An American Lyric*. Minneapolis: Graywolf Press, 2014.

Rilke, Rainer Maria. *Letters to a Young Poet*. 1929. New York: WW Norton, 2004.

Robertson, Lisa. *The Weather*. Vancouver: New Star Books, 2001.

Scofield, Gregory. "Sitting Down to Ceremony: an Interview with Gregory Scofield." With Tanis MacDonald. *Across Cultures, Across Borders: Canadian Aboriginal and Native American Literatures*. Eds. Paul DePasquale,

Renate Eigenbrod and Emma LaRocque. Peterborough: Broadview Press, 2010. 289–296.

Vonnegut, Kurt Jr. *A Man Without a Country*. Ed. Daniel Simon. New York: Seven Stories, 2006.

Winterson, Jeanette. *Why Be Happy When You Could Be Normal?* New York: Random House, 2011.

Zuehlke, Mark, and Louise Donnelly. *Magazine Writing from the Boonies*. Montreal and Kingston: McGill-Queen's University Press, 1996.

Originally from Winnipeg, Tanis MacDonald now lives in Waterloo, Ontario, where she teaches Canadian literature and creative writing at Wilfrid Laurier University. She won the Bliss Carman Poetry Prize in 2003, was a finalist for the Gabrielle Roy Prize in 2013 for her book *The Daughter's Way* and was the recipient of the Robert Kroetsch Teaching Award from the Canadian Creative Writers and Writing Programs in 2017 and the Faculty of Arts Teaching Scholar Award at WLU in 2018. She is co-editor (with Rosanna Deerchild and Ariel Gordon) of *GUSH: menstrual manifestos for our times* from Frontenac House. Widely published as a scholar and a reviewer, her fourth poetry book is coming out with Book*hug in Fall 2019.